PENGUIN BOOKS

COLLIDE

Tay Guan Hin, or 'Guan' as people know him, is a former tank mechanic, and the creative chairman of BBDO Singapore. He is also the founder and GCCO of TGH Collective.

As a former regional CCO in J Walter Thompson Asia Pacific, Guan has helped Shell, Johnson & Johnson, Abbott, P&G, HSBC, Unilever and other global brands to improve market share and solve complex business challenges.

He operates well within this complexity, always matching flawless execution with inspiring creative ideas and staying true to the brand's DNA.

A recipient of over 300 international, regional and local creative awards, Guan was fortunate enough to be recognized at Cannes Lions as a jury president for Outdoor—the first Asian in SEA to receive such an honour. He was also the first Asian to lead a prestigious global show called Design & Art Direction. He has been a jury president at Clio and at regional award shows like Asian Effies and Adfest.

Known to be a creative innovator, Guan has spoken at TEDx and been a global keynote speaker in many industry events like Spikes Asia, AD STAR in Korea, Adfest in Thailand, Brand Magic Summit in Mauritius, One Show in China/NY and Cannes Lions in France.

Guan also mentors young talents. He spoke and trained students in the 2004 One Show China and again in 2018, where he served as a judge and spoke at the One Show Greater China Creative Summit. Guan also set up the first advertising student awards in Singapore and was invited to be a Mentor for One Show China Youth Creative Awards 2019.

T0150639

'*Collide* empowers readers to harness their creativity in groundbreaking ways. A must-read for innovators everywhere!'
—Troy Ruhanen, President & CEO, TBWA/WORLDWIDE

'*Collide* is more than a guide; it's an invitation to break the barriers to our creativity. And when I say "break", I mean "break".'
—Andrew Robertson, President & CEO, BBDO WORLDWIDE

'*Collide* explores adopting conflict to stimulate creativity, demonstrating its vital role in generating innovative ideas. It demystifies the idea-creation process, presenting a clear blueprint for leveraging the power of creative conflict. The book highlights that while merging different ideas can be chaotic, this chaos leads to genuine innovation, opening doors to new possibilities and breakthrough discoveries.'
—Kevin Swanepoel, CEO, The One Club for Creativity

'This book is extremely helpful. And at the same time, a sacrilege! Because it reveals all the secrets that creative people have and teaches how to be creative. Thanks to Guan, it is now possible for any intelligent person to have great creative ideas themselves. He reveals all the techniques, regardless of himself and others who live on creative ideas. Now, joking aside, it's a wonderful book worth reading for creative people because it opens up completely new worlds—many thanks for this enlightening masterpiece.'
—Doerte Spengler-Ahrens, Chief Creative Officer, Jung von Matt SAGA, Art Directors Club President

'Wow, wow, wow, I absolutely loved *Collide*. From the amazing artwork to the playful tone to the impactful ideas and mind-expanding lessons, I know this will become a bestseller. A wonderful, practical and very insightful book that will far exceed its promise and make you a better person overall. What a rare treat of a read.'

—Andrea T Edwards, CSP,
Author of *Uncommon Courage: An Invitation*

'Do not pick up this book unless you are ready to be washed over with creativity and ideas. Readers have been warned. Guan has created a book that every creative thinker and doer needs.'

—Dr. Tanvi Gautam, MD Leadershift Inc.
Global HR Influencer, Keynote speaker,
Author of *Deep Collaboration* and *The Spark Lies Within*

'An exceptionally inspiring book, *Collide*, penned by an experienced storyteller. Guan imparts profound yet practical insights, making it a rare gem that resonates long after the last page. This book is an indispensable guide for anyone aspiring to impact creativity significantly. It goes beyond thinking outside the box—it's about inventing an entirely new box.'

—Ali Rez, Chief Creative Officer,
IMPACT BBDO Group MENAP

'Quirky, colourful and engaging from the word go—Guan takes you into the world of creativity. Buckle your seatbelt!'

—Simone Heng, Author of *Let's Talk About Loneliness*,
Human Connection Specialist

'What sets *Collide* apart is its ability to articulate the idea-generation process in a structured yet fun tone. It clarifies the often-chaotic brainstorming process, providing a framework that encourages the collision of ideas. Throughout the book, it reassures the reader that true innovation is rarely a neat process but requires the courage to explore uncharted territories.'

—Dr. Jerome Joseph, CSP & CEO,
The Global Brand Academy. Best-selling Author
and Ranked No. 2 in the world, Global Brand
Thought Leader, Consulting and Speaking
in thirty-seven countries

'Guan Hin brilliantly encapsulates what it means to be a true innovator: embracing the messiness of creative conflict to pursue breakthrough thinking. The book's dedication to fearless innovators mirrors my journey—from steering the marketing strategies at BMW Asia to establishing my own award-winning business. As someone who has faced considerable challenges, I resonate with the message that the path to innovation is fraught with obstacles, but overcoming these truly defines a phoenix-like spirit.'

—Sonja Piontek, CSP, Former Director of
Marketing BMW Asia, Best Selling Author,
Award Winning Thought Leader,
Acclaimed Global Keynote Speaker

'Wowza! I've known Guan since he was a young art director with a glimmer in his eye and have watched him rise through this business with immense passion, modesty, and talent. For him to crack open his brain and provide such a valuable tool for problem solving is a true gift to any professional who solves stuff for a living. Soak it in. This book is a bonafide masterclass in creativity. A must-read from one of the true class acts in this business. Two thumbs held so ridiculously high they could get a double nosebleed.'

—Cameron Day, Author of
The Advertising Survival Guide trilogy,
Creative Mentor, Fractional Code-cracker

'The concept of *Collide* in photography involves capturing spontaneous interactions and collisions of subjects, emotions, and environments. Guan's book presents this concept as a practical and enjoyable method; illustrating how true innovation arises from the clash of ideas.'

—Russel Wong, Hollywood Celebrity Photographer and Asia's most prolific fashion and portrait photographer; part of the elite group assigned to shoot covers for *Time* magazine

'Guan's creative conflict process is what leaders need to get past staid, conventional solutions for the challenges we face today. *Collide* does the job practically and effectively while creating new, insightful, attention-grabbing impact.'

—Joanne Flinn, Author of *Greensight: The Sustainability Guide for Company Directors*, Chairwoman of the ESG Institute

'Brace yourself for a whirlwind tour of creative rejuvenation! *Collide* is a powerful collection of practical tools to spark your creative flair and focus your brainstorming journey. With decades of experience and unrelenting excitement, Guan Hin shows you how to fuse conflicting ideas and emerge with tantalizing results.'

—Ron Kaufman, CEO of Uplifting Service, NYT Bestselling Author of *Uplifting Service*, Global Keynote Speaker, Ranked World's #1 Customer Experience Guru

'Conflict. It's scary. It's messy. It will reveal who you really are. And that's why it's the perfect ingredient for creativity. *Collide* demystifies creative thinking. The book shows us that while there is always a drop of magic and mystery on the creative journey, there are also very trusted pathways you can take to get there. Guan Hin reminds us that an appetite for adventure and the unexpected keeps your ideas alive. And . . . he also reminds us why so many of us have chosen—and keep choosing—the creative life.'

—Suhana Gordhan, Independent Creative Leader,
Executive Creative Director, Chief Aunty of
Young Creative

'*Collide* by Guan, dives into how conflict fuels creativity. It's a straightforward exploration of how clashes of ideas can lead to groundbreaking innovations. Guan uses clear, engaging examples to show how what seems like a hindrance can actually be a driving force in creative work. It's a must-read for creatives and brand strategists alike.'

—Uma Rudd Chia, Executive
Creative Director & Co-founder, KVUR

Collide

Embracing Conflict
to Boost Creativity

Tay Guan Hin

PENGUIN BOOKS

An imprint of Penguin Random House

PENGUIN BOOKS

USA | Canada | UK | Ireland | Australia
New Zealand | India | South Africa | China | Southeast Asia

Penguin Books is part of the Penguin Random House group of companies
whose addresses can be found at global.penguinrandomhouse.com

Published by Penguin Random House SEA Pte Ltd
9, Changi South Street 3, Level 08-01,
Singapore 486361

First published in Penguin Books by Penguin Random House SEA 2024
Copyright © Tay Guan Hin 2024

ISBN 9789815127119

Typeset in Garamond by MAP Systems, Bengaluru, India
Printed at Markono Print Media Pte Ltd, Singapore

www.penguin.sg

Dedication

To all the fearless innovators, champions of brainstorming, and brave souls who dare to dream big, this book is dedicated to you.

You embrace the messiness of creative conflict and are unafraid to break things in pursuit of breakthrough thinking. You refuse to settle for the status quo and constantly strive to push boundaries and challenge norms.

On your journey of creativity, may this book be your guide. May it give you the tools and framework to spark your imagination and help you generate problem-solving ideas. May it remind you that creative conflict is the world's most powerful ideation technique, and the secret behind every invention and innovation.

And most of all, may it inspire you to continue smashing ideas together, despite the dangers and risks that lie ahead. For it is in this messy, chaotic and unpredictable process, that true innovation is born.

Contents

Foreword

When I was growing up, I complained about my constant migraine headaches to my mom. You would expect her, like any other mom, to rummage through the drawers for some cure-for-all paracetamol tablets. Well, she didn't. My mom simply said, 'Dear, you have too many colliding thoughts in your head. Sort them out.'

Colliding thoughts. Early on, I knew that these are the seeds of every brilliant creative idea ever made. That's why I felt goosebumps when I started reading my friend Guan Hin's book. It elaborated on my mom's statement. It made me understand more about the process of ideation like no other. It gave meaning to my brain, and every single creative brain activity when trying to come up with ideas, or even solve problems.

Collide takes you on a double, triple loop of a roller-coaster ride of brainstorming tips, real-world examples and exciting inspiring stories. It shows how creative conflict has helped people and companies to innovate and succeed. I loved how he proves that conflict is not only good, but also necessary in generating and sparking creativity. He unapologetically tells us how messy this process can be, but at the same time, encourages us to embrace the chaos and take more risks.

If you're that person, creative or not, who is overwhelmed by problems that need solving, or afraid that maybe your ideas are not good enough or panicking that your deadline is in two hours and you have nothing to show, this book is for you.

And when you meet Guan Hin, thank him for the help. Because that's the first thing I'll do. As Tupac Shakur once rapped, *'You either ride wit' us, or collide wit' us'*. Guess it's time for us to collide.

Merlee Jayme

CHAIRMOM, Founder of The MISFITS CAMP:
A creative training camp for the Neurodiverse,
Former Chief Creative Officer at Dentsu Creative APAC,
International Speaker, Author, CNN Leading Women

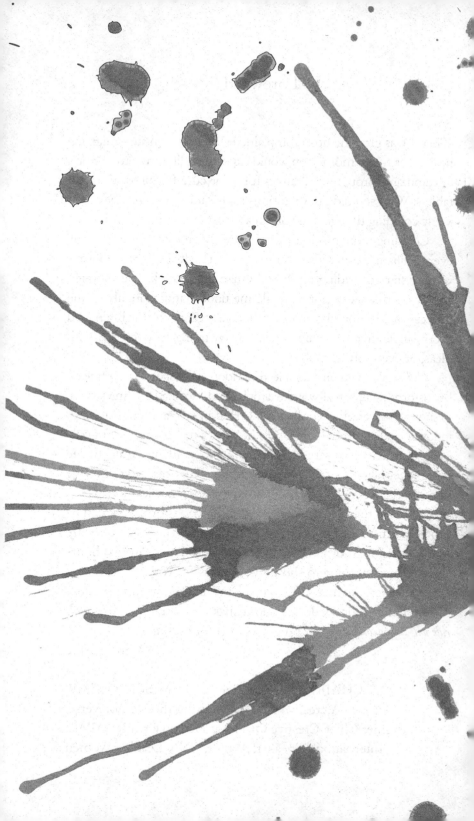

Chapter One

MUCH A DO A BOUT NOTHING

(Where I waffle on a bit about myself,
and why I wrote this book).

Introducing Me . . .
Your Friendly Guide to Making it Through This Ride Alive

Hello there, astute book purchaser! It's a great pleasure to meet someone as curious and as intelligent as you. Let me introduce myself.

My name is Guan (pronounced 'gwan', rhymes with 'barn'). I'm the creative chairman for an advertising agency called BBDO Singapore. My job is to be a brand storyteller for companies like Unilever, VISA, Nestlé and Shell. This means I help global brands improve their market share by solving complex business challenges.

For over thirty years, I've learnt how to create effective, productive and efficient ideas using 'creative conflict'. Today, I'm going to share these techniques with you. I'm going to bare everything—spill the beans—and reveal my secrets. And best of all, I'm going to turn you into an expert in using conflict to create ideas.

I'll be your ruggedly handsome guide on this thrilling trip, as we learn everything there is to know about the world's most powerful, and most dangerous, ideation technique. Some of these tips will be new to you, and others will simply be common sense. I have to warn you though. There are parts of this book that won't be pretty. Some pages will be shocking. Some will be dangerous. But rest assured, every page contains a technique or methodology I use on a daily basis.

My hope is that once you have finished this book, you will quickly realize you have learnt an effective, simple way to come up with great ideas. And that tomorrow, you will use these techniques to find great success in your own world.

We're Almost Ready For A Little Healthy Conflict. But it's Not Too Late to Back Out

We're about to begin, and I'll totally understand if you're getting cold feet. It's not too late to quietly close this book and go do something safer. Just the thought of coming up with ideas is nerve-wracking. And to do it using 'conflict' sounds positively mortifying. But I promise, if you stick with me until the end, then together, we will get through this alive and break the myth that coming up with good ideas is hard.

It might sound shocking to some people, but the simple truth is everyone has the ability to come up with powerful new ideas, as long as they know how to do it. *But how will learning to come up with better ideas benefit me?* That's a great question, and my answer to that question is simple. The techniques in this book will provide invaluable help to any adult who wants to master the most powerful way to solve problems. And that's a very useful skill anyone can use to make their lives, and the world, a better place.

You may find examples of creative conflict in this book that relate to marketing (since that is my realm of expertise), but I've also included many examples from other non-advertising experts. You will find business case studies from corporations; stories about how famous inventors and scientists solved problems; and many words of wisdom from writers, philosophers and creative geniuses. Because learning how to come up with ideas is not just for the artsy types—it's for everyone.

You could be an executive in the business world, wanting to improve your company's bottom line. Or you may be an entrepreneur wanting to invent a new solution to an old problem. Perhaps you're simply seeking fame and wealth? Or perhaps you want to pursue creative hobbies and need a proven way to improve your originality. Or maybe you're just like most people, and want to find solutions to everyday problems, like making household chores easier.

Whatever problems you are trying to solve, this book contains the techniques that will show you how to solve them using the immense power of innovation. I'm reminded of a great metaphor for the power of innovation: 'Build a better mousetrap, and the world will beat a path to your door'. This is a quote often misattributed to the American writer Ralph Waldo Emerson. (Spoiler alert, he never said it). What he actually wrote is, 'If a man has good corn or wood, or boards, or pigs, to sell, or can make better chairs or knives, crucibles or church organs, than anybody else, you will find a broad hard-beaten road to his house, though it be in the woods.'[1] It's a bit sexist, and not as impressive-sounding as the mousetrap quote, but it means roughly the same thing. Innovation is the key to success in business, as well as in life. And that is the main reason to read this book.

I want you to take advantage of the impressive brainpower you already possess, so that you can use it to make your life better. After you've finished this book, I want you to become the world's most talented problem-solver. And although many of the ideas in this book are filled with personal danger, hopefully most of you will survive, and those that do can have a little fun along the way.

Today I'm going to show you how to become an expert at 'creative conflict', the world's most powerful ideation technique. Today, you will learn how to 'collide'. Or to put it simply, you will learn the ways to come up with productive ideas that solve problems. But what does that really mean? And what can you expect to gain? We will get into the usefulness of creative conflict in the next chapter titled, 'What is creative conflict . . . and can I order it from Amazon?' But first, a little more about me.

I grew up in Singapore, a country with a fairly strict culture. It's the kind of place where you're expected to obey the rules and be the perfect child who doesn't rock the boat. On top of that, my family had high expectations for me. This probably had something to do with the fact my family—mother, father and brother—were all doctors. Well, you know what? I wasn't born to be a doctor. In school, I was very easily distracted and my grades sucked. This was disrupting my parents' plans for me to graduate from a well-known university to a high-paying medical or corporate job.

Then one day, the school principal called up my parents and asked them to come in for a meeting. I had been caught doodling, or as the principal put it, 'damaging the school's textbooks'. Surely this was the last straw. No doubt I was going to be expelled. Sheepishly, I went along with my parents to the meeting. I was shivering with fear.

Then something magical happened. To my surprise, instead of getting a scolding, the principal told my parents they should be proud of me. He said I had a real passion for art. And that this should be encouraged. You could have knocked me over with a feather.

That was the last day my parents tried to turn me into a doctor. And it was a day I learnt two important lessons. First, that a little conflict was all it took to disrupt the status quo (Thank you, doodles!). And second, with a little encouragement, anyone can embrace a new way of thinking. Staid principals. Strict parents. Anyone. Even you.

Whether you realize it or not, you already have the ability to come up with ideas using creative conflict. All humans do. We are all creative problem-solvers. I'm just here to show you the most powerful way of doing it. And to show you how to safely navigate the dangers that may arise along the way. And trust me, dangers *will* arise.

> *Conflict is the primary engine of creativity and innovation. People don't learn by staring into a mirror; people learn by encountering differences.*
>
> Ronald A. Heifetz [2]

As noted above in the quote by Heifetz, I too have learned that encountering differences and difficulties has been the catalyst for personal development and opportunities; likely this has been the same for you, even if you haven't viewed it as such.

Conflict sparks creativity in ways that change the way we do things. In violent convulsions, conflict births new ideas that, in turn, create new realities. Indeed, throughout history, conflict has been the most critical tool for innovation, discovery and invention. But to many people, conflict is a scary idea. It sounds violent and dangerous and something usually best avoided. There is an old Japanese saying that translates in English to 'the nail that sticks out gets hammered down'. This saying expresses the fear all humans share of being ostracized for being different. And it's precisely this kind of fearful thinking that stops us from solving problems.

Fear is, without a doubt, the biggest obstacle we face when coming up with ideas. For some people who aren't as brave as we are, fear is an insurmountable hurdle. It stops them from ever trying to achieve anything. This is hardly surprising. As humans, we all share a fear of change, and a love of inertia. We are all scared of wasting time and money. Scared of failure. *What if I can't think of any good ideas? What if I have no creative talent? What if everyone laughs at me?*

These fears and anxieties are quite natural. You wouldn't be human if you didn't feel them. But luckily, they are all easily defeated by the most important skill you already possess. A passionate belief in yourself. Some people think you need talent to succeed. But talent is overrated. Talent has limits. Passion will always beat talent, because when you have passion, you continue to learn and grow.

Leo Burnett, probably one of the most famous advertising practitioners of the twentieth century is thought to have said: 'When you reach for the stars, you may not quite get one, but you won't come up with a handful of mud either.' It was actually said by his copy director John Crawford, but Burnett 'borrowed' the line and it became his agency's mantra.[3] And that line holds the secret to ideation success. Making sure you aim high with passion.

Later in this book, I will teach you a bunch of tricks. And show you how to discover powerful and innovative solutions to any problems you might be facing. You will learn about creative conflict. What is it? Why is it important? And how does it work? By the end of this book, you will have all the tools you need to smash ideas together like a professional.

But none of that will matter if you don't approach your own ideation sessions with passion. You have to reach for the stars. Ignore the fear. Take a chance. And believe in yourself. Remember, the fear that wants to stop you, can only be defeated by your passion to succeed. So be brave, my friend. Be courageous.

Anyway, it's getting late, and our journey has begun. Tread carefully, as the way forward is fraught with peril. I can't promise you'll get through this book unscathed. There may be a few sticky situations. Perhaps even a paper cut or two. But for those who make it through alive, you will learn how to spark creativity, ignite innovation and transform organizations.

Our adventure awaits—let's begin.

Stay Hydrated

When learning to collide ideas, you will need these fluids

Blood ✓
Sweat ✓
Tears ✓

*Conflict is the beginning
of consciousness.*

M. Esther Harding [4]

Chapter Two

YOU'RE ON A COLLISION COURSE

(Where I explain how creative conflict makes powerful new ideas)

What is Creative Conflict

In its simplest form, creative conflict is the process of finding new ideas by mashing-up old ideas. That's it. You've learned the secret. Thanks for buying the book.

Oh, you're still here. Well, I guess I better explain it then.

Ever since our little blue planet came into existence, progress has been a by-product of biological, cultural and physical conflict. From chemicals reacting together in the primordial ooze, to the endless clash of civilizations, conflict is the fuel that drives change. All of our inventions, breakthroughs and discoveries have been driven by conflict. In fact, all great ideas are built upon the embers of destruction. The current way of doing things must be destroyed so that new ways of doing them can rise phoenix-like from the ashes. Progress demands renewal.

Creative conflict is simply a means to an end. A process to help our brains make connections between seemingly unrelated ideas to form new ideas. Whether you're staring at a screen, or a blank sheet of paper, it's hard to have an original thought. Some would say impossible. But when you start colliding ideas together, something magical happens. Your brain starts to see connections where none existed before, and new outcomes are found. If your mind is observant, inspiration will strike. Even failed attempts can be illuminating. Colliding ideas together is the key.

Some people think they can't do it. They say things like, 'I'm not creative. That's for the "creative types".' Luckily for clever people, like you and me, we don't believe that nonsense. With the right training, we know that everyone is clever enough to come up with new ideas by mashing up old ideas.

Once you have become proficient in this technique of using creative conflict, you will begin to change the world. But don't forget one important thing. There's an AI program somewhere in the world that's also learning this technique. The race is on, puny human.

Interview with CREATIVITY EXPERT
Fredrik Härén

Before we begin, let's hear it from a global expert in creative conflict. Fredrik Härén is a world-famous author and speaker on business creativity known as The Creativity Explorer. He has interviewed thousands of creative people around the world to discover the secrets to how we can all become more creative.

Delivering over 2,000 presentations, lectures and workshops in over seventy countries, he has inspired millions of business people to become more creative, and to look at the world in a new way. He is the author of ten books, including *The Idea Book*, which was included in the 100 Best Business Books of All Time.

Guan: *Hi Fredrik. You're acknowledged as a global expert in creative thinking. When did you first discover how to crash ideas together to make new ones?*
Fredrik: For over twenty-five years, I have looked at creativity as learning how to combine knowledge and information in unexpected ways. From a very early age, I was fascinated by creativity and ideas. My brothers and I would invent new games, rewrite the rules and then play them again. I especially remember 'Schattack', a mix of Chess and Risk that we created.

Guan: *How would you describe the process of creative conflict?*
Fredrik: The creative process is not a struggle; it's a journey. To me, conflict is not a negative word.

Guan: *How important is creative conflict in the creative process?*
Fredrik: The most interesting answers are found where there is friction.

Guan: *What's your favourite brainstorming technique to collide ideas?*
Fredrik: Travel—for sure! I have interviewed some of the most respected CEOs in the world, as well as some of the poorest people on the planet for my research—research that has taken me from the deserts of Oman to the innovation labs in Silicon Valley. I have learned from respected Japanese sushi masters, famous European car designers, flamenco dancers in Spain, paper artists in Thailand, musicians in Holland and heads of innovation around the world, just to give a few examples. I am convinced that we can find more creativity in so many places.

Guan: *What's the purpose of mashing different ideas together?*
Fredrik: To give birth to something new. When things collide, new things are born.

Guan: *What's the hardest part of learning to mash up ideas?*
Fredrik: Learning to get rid of the 'truths' that we already have.

Guan: *Robots and apps are taking over our jobs. What creative skills do companies require in their current human employees?*
Fredrik: In 1993, while studying at university, I was introduced to the Internet for the first time and I instantly understood it would change the world as we knew it. Artificial intelligence is the same. In my words, AI stands for 'Additional Intelligence'. Suddenly we have access to some really smart help. But people need to be inspired to tap into this power. So the skill needed is the desire to re-learn how to think and create.

Guan: *What can I do to train my brain to think that way?*
Fredrik: Put yourself in unusual situations where you are not the expert. Being a newbie at something makes it easy

to re-learn. You can also train your brain in imaginative ways as well. I like to use a technique I call Blank Ideation. This is when you let yourself ideate an idea all the way, without ever thinking of executing it. Like you are shooting blanks. The purpose is not to 'hit' something; it's to practise the process, and to practise the art and skill of developing ideas. So when you do get a great idea that you want to take all the way to a finished product, you are already used to the process.

Guan: *How do you create a culture of collaboration within a company?*
Fredrik: You should focus on building a culture where people are curious.

Guan: *What advice would you give to someone learning about creative conflict?*
Fredrik: Do not be afraid of conflict. You need it to reach your full potential. I believe in the potential of humanity, and in the infinite power of human creativity. I am driven to help as many people as possible discover their full creative potential. And I think that the world would be a much better place if more people were given the chance to be more creative—and if they learned to pick up the best ideas that are generated around the world.

Guan: *Thank you, Fredrik.*

We've just heard from a global expert in creative thinking who believes strongly in the power of creative conflict. He knows *'creativity is learning how to combine knowledge and information in unexpected ways'* and he knows *'when things collide, new things are born'*. The short name for these combinations is *'mash-ups'*. Let's find out all about them on the next page.

What Mash-ups Look Like

As we've learnt in the previous interview with Fredrik Härén, when ideas collide, they give birth to something new. These colliding ideas are known as 'mash-ups', and they are the key to finding new ideas. But what do mash-ups look like in the real world? As luck would have it, you don't have to look far to see examples of creative conflict in our daily lives. Mash-ups are everywhere, from the Swiss Army Knife to the Spork. All around the world, innovators of all kinds, produce new ideas using creative conflict. We see it most obviously in food, music and digital technology.

From the multi-ethnic Peranakan cuisine found in Malaysia, to the Tex-Mex style found in Texas, USA, you will find fusion dishes in every country in the world. The classic Indian dish, *vindalho,* originated in Goa, India. But it's actually a local version of a Portuguese stew, *carne de vinha d'alhos.* The Vietnamese sandwich, *bánh mì,* is made using a short French baguette. And even the quintessential British meal, *fish and chips,* was first introduced to England by Jewish immigrants from Portugal and Spain.

Mash-ups, samples and remixes have always played a large role in the world of music. One of my favourites is 'Avicii vs Rick Astley—Never Gonna Wake You Up' (NilsOfficial Mashup) by NilsOfficial. This artist takes a modern beat (from Avicii), combines it with a famous older song (from Rick Astley) and adds a hook from a third song '*Chumbawamba*'. The last time I looked on YouTube, it had over 24 million views. Check it out. It's a banger.

In the digital world, almost every invention is a mash-up of technologies that existed before. Smartphones are probably the ultimate mash-up. They aren't just used to communicate; they are also TVs, internet browsers, radios, maps, video game systems, alarm clocks, photo albums, music players, cameras and much, much more.

They mash-up multiple technologies including GPS chips, gyroscopes, accelerometers, light sensors, Wi-Fi antennas and compasses, all run by a Central Processing Unit. This magical device does practically everything. And if it doesn't, I'm sure there's an app for that.

Using mash-ups to create new technologies isn't even a modern technique. Ever since our distant ancestors combined a sharpened rock with a stick to make a spear, mash-ups have been used to create new tools, inventions and ideas. When wheels were combined with rivers, watermills were created that used hydropower to grind flour. In 1919, when an American named Edwin George combined an internal combustion engine with a rotary push mower, the modern lawnmower was born.

Hybrid cars are another example of a mash-up that has existed much longer than you'd imagine. Way back in 1901, Ferdinand Porsche (yes, that Porsche) created the Lohner-Porsche Mixte Hybrid, the first car to combine petrol and electric motors. There are many theories (conspiracy and otherwise) as to why these didn't become popular, but it wasn't until 1997 that Toyota launched the first mass-market hybrid car, the very popular *Prius*.

In today's world, it's almost impossible to find an invention that doesn't combine several technologies. Noise-cancelling headphones are a good example. In 1978, Dr Amar Bose (the founder of the famous audio company) was on a flight to Europe, when he noticed he couldn't enjoy the music from his headphones due to the roar of the aeroplane engines. His solution was to combine headphones with noise-cancelling technology. This technology works by analysing ambient sounds and then neutralizing them by transmitting a mirror-image sound wave. If you've ever used one on a flight, you know how well they work.

Mash-up inventions can be found absolutely everywhere. Industrial machines such as bulldozers are a mash-up of tractors and military tank treads. Cronuts are a mash-up of doughnuts and croissants. We have amphibious cars which are a mash-up of cars and boats. And we have seaplanes, which are a mash-up of planes and boats. Even the humble E-bike is a mash-up of a bicycle, a battery and an electric motor.

From simply entertaining to world-changing, mash-ups are found in every part of our lives. The best kind of mash-up reframes the original narrative to produce a fresh perspective. By appropriating existing ideas and reinterpreting them, we can create something new that is a hybrid of both. Soon, you will be using this technique to come up with new ideas. Just imagine the incredible things you'll create, when you start colliding using creative conflict. That is, if the robots don't get there first.

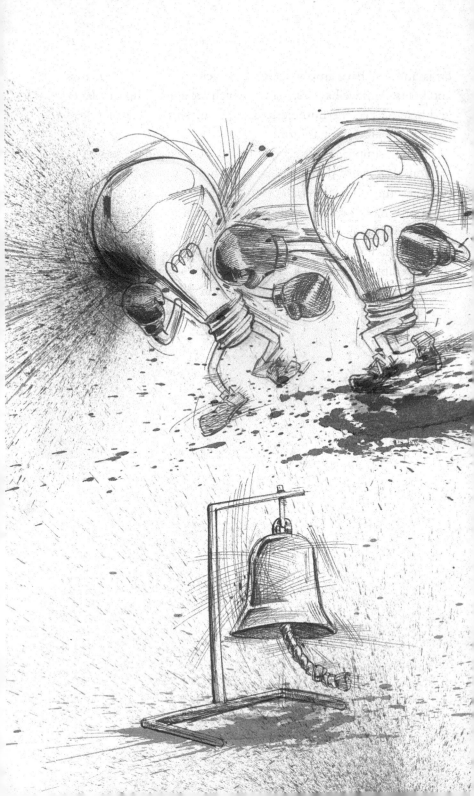

*Creativity comes from
a conflict of ideas.*

Donatella Versace [5]

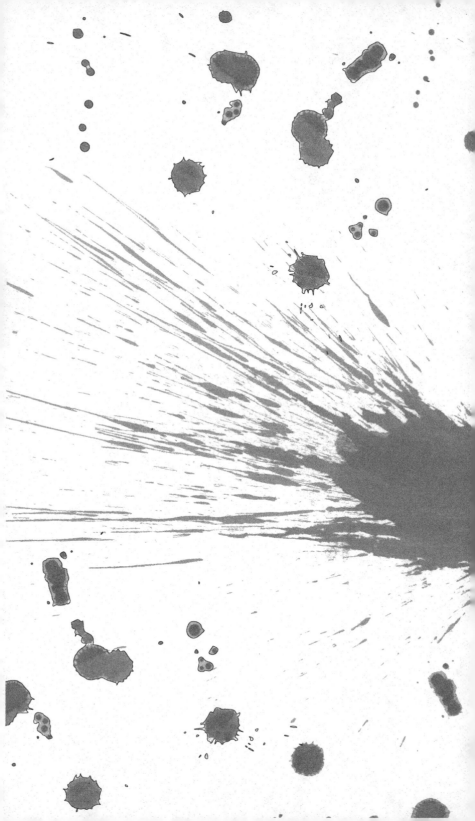

Chapter Three

THE ROBOTS ARE COMING

(Where I discuss why creative conflict
is the key to surviving extinction)

Don't Turn the Page . . .
They're Watching Us

I need to tell you something quickly. Are you sitting down? Feeling comfortable? Try not to overreact—and I don't want to freak you out—but the robots have arrived. And they're taking our jobs.

After the industrial revolution, humans had to learn to work with machines. Today, we follow work practices dictated by algorithms. What kind of work will be available for humans in the future? It's a timely question. If the robots can do almost everything already, what kind of jobs will be left for us mere mortals? As it happens, creative conflict holds some of the answers.

According to the world's leading economists, we're in the Fourth Industrial Revolution. The business world is changing faster than most people can adapt. Our roles in the economy are changing in ways we can't predict, and people are wondering what the future might look like. In 2020, the World Economic Forum's *Future of Jobs Report* outlined the challenges that lie ahead. Importantly, they noted that as new technologies are adopted, 50 per cent of all employees would need reskilling by 2025.[6] There's an even chance this includes you.

We are in a period of rapid change. But before our robot overlords take full control, we humans will need to acquire new skills in the near future to remain useful and productive. Creative conflict isn't just a way to find problem-solving ideas; it's also a method of thinking that will give you some of the most important skills needed in the coming years. Join me now, as we take a short trip into the imminent future.

THE TOP TEN
SKILLS IN 2025

 Analytical thinking and innovation

 Active learning and learning strategies

 Complex problem-solving

 Critical thinking and analysis

 Creativity, originality and initiative

 Leadership and social influence

 Technology use, monitoring and control

 Technology design and programming

 Resilience, stress tolerance and flexibility

 Reasoning, problem-solving and ideation

Icons by flaticon.com

Source: World Economic Forum, 'The Future of Jobs' Report, 2020.

Welcome to the Future

How are you feeling? Was the time jump painful? I hope the journey wasn't too awkward. We're still working on the technology to allow you to time travel with your clothes on. So take this towel for now and follow me. I'd like to show you something really interesting.

This is the year 2025. Regrettably, flying cars have still not been invented, but many other things have changed, especially in the workplace. As you can see in this chart on the left-hand page, the skills needed by today's employees look very different from the ones from the past. Six of the skills highlighted (including the top five) use creative conflict.

Gone are the old days where jobs had physical requirements and involved memorizing and regurgitating data. Now what's important is how you think and engage with technology. As the World Economic Forum predicted in 2020, creative conflict is the key to surviving the workplace of today (your imminent future).

Creative conflict helps you become an expert in organic ways of thinking and processing information. Finding connections that don't exist, according to logic. And as far as we know, Artificial Intelligence (AI) has not perfected this organic way of thinking. Yet.

Creative conflict is not just a powerful ideation tool; it's the key to your survival. This will be handy once you've learnt it. After all, you don't want to end up like the dinosaurs. Now it's time to head back to the recent past. You can leave the towel here.

Rise of the Machines

There's been a lot of doom and gloom recently about the rise of the machines. Specifically, AI.

As anyone who hasn't been living under a rock has realized, AI is making remarkable progress in many fields. A prominent development is the emergence of language processing tools like ChatGPT and Midjourney that generate human-like text and images. Many people are calling these tools the end of creativity. But is creative conflict really on its deathbed? Are creative thinkers all doomed? Not even in the slightest. And I'll tell you why. This has all happened before. You just don't remember it.

Way back in the nineteenth century, visual artists made their careers by how realistically they could paint. Then in 1839, a revolutionary technology was created. It was a new, high-tech means of visual representation that could represent reality more accurately than any humble painter. They called it . . . photography.

The French painter Paul Delaroche is thought to have said, 'From today, painting is dead!' And for a short time, everyone thought it was. And then a magical thing happened. The rise of the camera spurred artists such as Camille Pissarro, Claude Monet and Pierre Auguste Renoir to create a new way of looking at the world. Collectively, they were known as the Impressionists. They were soon joined by new art movements like Cubism, Expressionism, Surrealism, Abstraction and many more. Rather than killing the art of painting, photography freed artists from the representational prison they had been painting in. And painting was reborn.

AI has the power to free us in the same way. The advertising industry already uses AI for rapid prototyping of artistic concepts, creating original content, brainstorming visual ideas and producing ads automatically, making advertising more efficient. But it can't create anything by itself. It still needs a human brain to have the idea in the first place. AI can only replace the tedious part of creation by scouring billions of words and pictures, to find solutions that are technically astounding in their detail.

AI might be the world's most powerful mimic, but it's as smart as a box of hammers. It will never be able to work like an organic brain. Your brain is literally unique in its processing power, experiences, motivation, ideas and passion. Your ideas are unique to you, and cannot be replicated by AI. Mimicked? Yes. But can never be created without a human.

Even if we reach the technological singularity, where AI becomes sentient and starts doing its own thing, it will still not overtake us, because its ideas will be the product of logic, not human experience. It can't create the kinds of illogical, counterintuitive and unique thoughts that your brain can make. It can't solve problems, by finding connections that don't already exist, like your brain can. Of course, one day, a super-intelligent AI may decide to kill us all. But that's a different discussion for another day.

One of the most intriguing aspects of AI is its ability to generate unexpected responses. It can learn from vast amounts of data, to create text and images that are not limited by preconceived notions or biases. AI's creative potential lies in its ability to generate content that is different from what humans might produce. This can provide a fresh perspective on a problem and stimulate creative thinking.

Creative conflict, on the other hand, throws individuals with different perspectives and ideas together in a dialogue to generate new solutions or ideas. It involves challenging assumptions, questioning beliefs, and exploring different perspectives to arrive at a more innovative solution. Creative conflict breaks down rigid thinking patterns and encourages collaboration and innovation.

By combining AI and creative conflict, companies can generate a more diverse range of ideas and perspectives. This leads to more effective solutions and helps them adapt to changing circumstances. As AI technologies continue to evolve, it is important to explore their potential to enhance creativity and innovation. By embracing these technologies and leveraging creative conflict, companies can remain competitive in today's rapidly changing world.

Just as machines ease soul-destroying work, replacing obsolete thinking, everyone today has information sources built on outstanding knowledge. And while AI can replace time-consuming jobs, it can never replace the way humans process that knowledge.

It still takes a human brain to engage in creative conflict, create a new idea, and recognize a good idea. So give your brain a nice, warm hug. It's smarter and more powerful than AI. And much prettier too.

Interview with **ROBOT OVERLORD** ChatGPT

At this point, it might be enlightening to hear what an AI expert has to say about creative conflict. Or it might not. That's right, I spoke to ChatGPT itself. As we all know, ChatGPT is an AI language model. It's not human. So when I asked it my usual questions, it gave me some decidedly non-human answers. That's probably because I asked it to be as creative as possible and to have fun. My mistake. It led to answers that contained a little bit of wisdom, and a whole lot of weirdness. Some answers were surreal, most were completely untrue, but a couple were comedy gold. Without further ado, let's hear what our future robot overlord has to say about creative conflict.

Guan: *Hello ChatGPT. Can you describe the process of creative conflict?*
ChatGPT: Creative conflict is like a culinary battle royale, where ideas are the ingredients, and arguments are the seasonings. It's like the chaos in a kitchen of clashing chefs, whipping up a storm of innovation, with the fire of disagreement and the spice of contrasting perspectives. It's a wild ride of tossing, mixing and taste-testing until the perfect creative dish emerges, ready to be served.

Guan: *Your cooking analogy is entertaining, but not quite right. Let me ask another question. How vital is creative conflict to the creative process?*
ChatGPT: Creative conflict is as vital to the creative process as oxygen is to fire. No fire, no heat; no creative conflict, no breakthroughs. Creative conflict is as vital as a llama is to a tightrope walker. It might seem unnecessary, but without that llama pushing boundaries, the act just wouldn't be as captivating.

Guan: *Your first analogy about oxygen and fire is spot on. The llama reference is not. How important is disruption?*
ChatGPT: Disruption is like a caffeine shot to the world, jolting us awake and energizing us to reimagine what's possible. Disruption is as important as a penguin at a pool party. Sure, the party would go on without it, but the penguin adds that extra flair that makes it unforgettable.

Guan: *Your description of disruption is funny, but wildly off the mark. I'll try another question. What's the purpose of mashing different ideas together?*
ChatGPT: Mashing different ideas together is like making a smoothie with unconventional ingredients; sometimes it's delicious, sometimes it's terrible, but it's always a surprising treat. It's like throwing paint on a canvas, creating a vibrant masterpiece of innovation. It's a beautiful mess that leads to brilliant discoveries, much like the time Jackson Pollock accidentally spilled his coffee and created modern art.

Guan: *Wow. Robot humour can be quite sarcastic. I'm really regretting asking you to be as creative as possible. Tell me, what's the hardest part of learning to mash up ideas?*
ChatGPT: The most challenging part of mashing up ideas is overcoming the fear of creating a Frankenstein's monster, that's equal parts brilliant and bizarre. It's like trying to tame a wild unicorn with a spoon—it's an unpredictable endeavour that requires a delicate balance of skill, persistence and imagination. Mashing up ideas is like trying to knit with spaghetti. It's slippery and messy, and it takes a whole lot of patience to create something beautiful.

Guan: *Finally, a reasonably good answer. Mashing up ideas is scary, unpredictable and takes imagination. What can I do to train my brain to think of mash-ups?*

ChatGPT: To train your brain for creative mash-ups, try mental gymnastics. Do crossword puzzles in crayon or listen to opera while breakdancing—shake up your synapses! Try doing daily puzzles while riding a unicycle. It's all about balancing chaos and order—just like your morning commute. Consider learning to juggle flaming swords while riding a unicycle on a tightrope—it's a practice in managing chaos and turning it into something extraordinary.

Guan: *None of that answer is true. What are your favourite techniques to collide ideas?*

ChatGPT: As an AI language model, I don't have personal preferences, but I can create fictional scenarios based on your request. One brainstorming technique to collide ideas is the 'Pinball Wizard'—you bounce ideas around like a pinball, ricocheting off each other, scoring points for creativity and, occasionally, getting stuck in the bonus round. Another brainstorming technique to collide ideas is 'Speed Dating for Concepts': pairing random ideas for a quick, intense exploration of their chemistry. Another technique is 'Pin the Idea on the Donkey.' You blindfold yourself, spin around, and let the creative darts fly. It's a winning combination of childhood games and innovation.

Guan: *I like 'Speed Dating for Concepts'. The rest? Not so much. Have you ever seen a great 'fish-out-of-water' solution?*

ChatGPT: As an AI language model, I don't have personal experiences or the ability to observe situations. However, I can provide you with a fictional 'fish-out-of-water' solution when an accountant used their number-crunching skills to help a fashion designer create a clothing line, based on mathematical patterns. Talk about a fashionable formula! Another solution I've seen was when a sushi chef fixed a broken bicycle chain with a pair of chopsticks—it might not have been the traditional approach, but it got the wheels turning.

Guan: *Those are interesting stories, but I think they refer more to lateral thinking solutions. Have you ever created an advertising campaign using creative conflict?*

ChatGPT: Unfortunately, being an AI language model, I don't have personal experiences. However, I can create fictional scenarios based on your request. My best campaign solution using creative conflict was when I facilitated a rap battle between marketing teams, igniting an epic lyrical war that generated a tagline for the ages. Unfortunately, as an AI language model, I can't provide a case study for that campaign. But feel free to use the rap battle anecdote as inspiration. Another solution using creative conflict was when I combined elements of a detective novel with a cooking show. The result? A mouthwatering mystery that had audiences craving for more.

Guan: *Those fictional solutions made with creative conflict were terrible. Let me try a different question. Currently, robots like you are taking over our jobs. What skills will companies require from human employees?*

ChatGPT: Companies need human employees with the creative skills of a chameleon. They must adapt, camouflage, and have a 360-degree vision to outperform the metallic competition. Human employees are needed with the creativity of a toddler given free rein in a paint store, the adaptability of a chameleon on a disco ball, and the resilience of a rubber duck in a tsunami.

Guan: *Companies do need employees to be creative, adaptable and resilient. And your analogies were entertaining. So then, how do you create a culture of collaboration?*

ChatGPT: To create a culture of collaboration within a company, nurture a petri dish of diversity, trust and open communication, cultivating the growth of teamwork organisms. Collaboration is like hosting a potluck dinner for ideas. Encourage everyone to bring their best dish to the table and sample each other's delectable contributions.

Guan: *That's a great answer too. Diversity, trust and open communication are very important. Are there any dangers when collaborating?*
ChatGPT: Collaboration's dark side can breed groupthink, dilute originality and sometimes transform brainstorming sessions into chaotic battlegrounds. The dangers of collaboration include the potential for creating a Frankenstein's monster of ideas—a patchwork creation that may come to life, but ultimately terrifies everyone involved. It's like a game of Jenga. Build too high without a solid foundation, and the whole tower of ideas can come crashing down.

Guan: *Groupthink and unfocused brainstorming are definitely two of the dangers. When collaborating to solve problems, what's the most important thing to remember?*
ChatGPT: When problem-solving with creative conflict, remember: the goal is to wrestle with ideas, not each other. It's a battleground of ideas, so bring your best armour and a sense of humour. It's like navigating a room full of banana peels—staying on your feet requires a combination of agility, humour and the ability to laugh at yourself.

Guan: *I love that answer, 'wrestle with ideas, not each other'. I'm stealing that. Tell me, can data analysis help the mash-up process of ideation?*
ChatGPT: Data analysis is like a microscope for ideation, helping us zoom in on the hidden connections and patterns that spark innovative mash-ups. Using data analysis in the mash-up process is like having a personal DJ for your ideation playlist. It helps you find the perfect beat to make your ideas dance together.

Guan: *You're right. It is important to find hidden connections and patterns in the data. But the DJ stuff is just gobbledygook. How important is reviewing and testing ideas before implementing them?*
ChatGPT: Reviewing and testing ideas is as important as trying on a pair of pants before buying them—you might think they'll fit, but you won't know for sure until you've jumped, danced and done a few lunges. Reviewing and testing ideas is like a game of whack-a-mole. You'll have to knock down a few, before you find the one that pops up as the winner.

Guan: *Great analogy with the pants. I might steal that one too. What advice would you give to someone just beginning to learn about creative conflict?*
ChatGPT: Treat it like a rollercoaster ride: it might be scary at first, but once you embrace the twists and turns, you'll find yourself enjoying the adrenaline rush. Embrace the chaos like a surfer riding a tsunami—it might be overwhelming at first, but learning to ride the wave will take you to new heights. For someone learning about creative conflict, my advice is: embrace the chaos, dance in the fire and remember—diamonds are formed under pressure.

Guan: *Inspiring advice. I agree. Thanks, ChatGPT.*

As you can tell by the surreal and, sometimes, nonsensical answers, it's best not to ask ChatGPT to be as creative as possible and have fun with the answers. While it did have a few snippets of wisdom and a few good analogies, it definitely had trouble coming up with examples of creative conflict that used innovative, workable solutions and human insights. Instead, it offered a lot of poorly formed puns, and cliché motivational poster thoughts. It did teach me one new thing though. I am definitely getting a penguin for my next pool party!

As for you, dear reader, you'll notice this interview has just demonstrated that AI is still an imperfect tool. Sure, it can help describe creative conflict, but it can't do it for us. Our organic way of thinking is still needed. For the time being, humans rule.

Dinosaurs Go Extinct

Why is creative conflict so important to the way we do business? Quite simply, it's a powerful tool to create new ideas, and innovation is the critical skill that's needed now, and into the future. The businesses that will thrive in the future are those that can adapt fastest, and innovate faster with better ideas. Those that can't adapt, will perish.

History is littered with the remains of once-great companies that failed to innovate. Companies like Pan Am, Borders and Blockbuster. These were companies that were once staffed by forward-thinking innovators, who then failed to adapt to a changing business environment. What happened to them? Let's find out.

In the world of aviation, Pan American World Airways, or Pan Am, was an iconic symbol of twentieth-century air travel. It was the first airline to fly worldwide, and pioneered many innovations, including the use of jumbo jets and computerized reservation systems. It made global travel accessible, and defined the golden age of aviation. Pan Am was so famous, its planes were used in three James Bond films and a fictional Pan Am 'spaceplane' appeared in Stanley Kubrick's *2001: A Space Odyssey*.

However, Pan Am's failure to adapt and innovate in the face of growing competition led to its demise. As deregulation swept the industry, Pan Am made several mistakes. It lacked a strong domestic feeder network and was too dependent on international routes. High operating costs, fluctuating fuel prices and geopolitical crises, all helped to erode profits. In 1991, the once-pioneering airline filed for bankruptcy. The end of Pan Am is a powerful lesson in the dangers of failing to adapt to changing conditions.[7]

If you're a lover of books, you may remember that once upon a time, the best retail bookseller in the world was a company called Borders.

The company started in America in 1971 and quickly became nationally and internationally popular. They were famous for their extensive inventory, in-store ambience and knowledgeable staff. They popularized the superstore concept, making reading and buying books a fun, communal experience.

Sadly, for Borders, the creation of digital and online platforms spelled disaster. Despite its forty-year history of innovation in physical retailing, Borders lagged behind in the digital revolution. The company's inability to innovate and adapt to the shift towards e-commerce and digital reading platforms, helped destroy the company. Increasing operational costs and decreasing in-store sales put the company under financial stress until, eventually, it filed for bankruptcy in 2011. The sad demise of Borders is a poignant reminder of the inevitability of change, and the necessity of innovation in the face of industry disruption.[8]

The last dinosaur I want to mention is Blockbuster Video. Before the internet was invented, if you didn't feel like watching a new movie at the cinema, you could always head down to your local Blockbuster Video and rent a movie to watch at home. The company was the number one rental chain in the 1990s, with thousands of stores worldwide offering a vast selection of movies. Blockbuster revolutionized the home entertainment industry, but like the other companies I've mentioned, it failed to adapt to emerging technologies.

The downfall began when Netflix introduced its DVD-by-mail service, followed by online streaming, which Blockbuster underestimated. The rise of digital media and streaming platforms rendered their physical rental model obsolete. Because Blockbuster ignored the birth of the digital age, the company faced financial losses, store closures and, ultimately, bankruptcy.[9]

These three failed companies, and others like them, teach us that innovation is the key to survival. And that applies to people as much as it does to companies. As we have learned from the

'Future of Jobs' report, employers are looking for people with critical thinking and problem-solving skills. They need people who know how to harness creative conflict for innovation. And they need people who can collaborate and work effectively in teams of diverse groups, with opposing points of view.

At every level of business, creative conflict is the key. It teaches you to think quickly, creatively and analytically. It enables faster, more efficient thinking. And leads to more effective ideas that deliver better results. Employees who have creative conflict skills will be very valuable to the employer of the present, as well as the future.

There are many other reasons to learn the secrets of creative conflict. After all, learning to 'collide' also makes your brain work better. But my favourite reason for learning creative conflict is simple. It enables you to stay off the Endangered Species list.

Technology is characterized by constant change, rapid innovation, creative destruction and revolutionary products.

Marsha Blackburn [10]

Chapter Four

THE POINT OF NO RETURN

(Where I give you one last warning
before you fall down the rabbit hole).

A Crash Course in Thinking

Hopefully, by now, you have a good understanding of what creative conflict is. Soon, it will be time to learn how to do it. But first, we need to get you ready.

It won't be pain-free, but we need to begin by exchanging your brain for a fresh one. Then, after your new brain has been installed, I will teach you how to collide well with others. After that, I'm going to reveal a set of dangerously powerful ideation techniques to help you crash ideas together. Finally, if you're not too injured to continue, I'll teach you to become a champion of C.O.L.L.I.D.E. *What's that?* I hear you ponder. C.O.L.L.I.D.E. is the name for seven-step process I follow when I want to create problem-solving ideas. More on that later.

Changing your brain—or changing the way you think—will change the way you work and help you discover new ways to solve problems. You will learn how to overcome the common barriers to creative thinking. You will learn the tools to generate new ideas, and gain the mindset to take creative leaps. You will grow your creative confidence by learning practical tools to break creative blocks. And you will discover how to create the right environment that unlocks the creative potential in your ideation team.

This will arm you with powerful creative problem-solving skills that will last a lifetime. And best of all, you will develop the one insatiable quality of geniuses—how to be permanently curious. Machines haven't learnt how to do that. Yet.

But one last warning. Once you learn these techniques, your brain will be changed forever. There really is no going back. So make a will. Kiss a loved one. And let's get started.

I have no special talent. I am only passionately curious.

Albert Einstein [11]

Interview with **PHILIPPINE MASTER** David Guerrero

We're almost ready to change the way you think, but first let's hear from one of the Philippines' top experts in creative thinking. David Guerrero is the creative chairman of BBDO Guerrero, consistently one of the most awarded advertising agencies in Asia. David has won Grand Prix for both Creativity and Effectiveness for clients including Pepsi, P&G, and the Philippine Department of Tourism. He has won hundreds of international awards and judged at AdFest, AdStars, Clio, D&AD, LIA, One Show and Spikes. He was the first from South-East Asia to be appointed Jury President at Cannes Lions. In 2020, David was re-elected Chairman of the Association of Accredited Advertising Agencies Philippines (4As).

Guan: *In the age of robots, how important is it for humans to think creatively?*
David: This is an interesting challenge. Generative AI tools like ChatGPT became quite famous in 2023 and sparked a lot of debate about what makes us different. There is a lot to concern us here, as automation and technology have, until now, been replacing manual, repetitive tasks while leaving mental and creative tasks for desk-bound thinkers. Now we have to re-think that, and see how we can stay a step ahead. Just as in technological revolutions before, what has survived is the highest quality work. In a world of mass production, we value handcrafted wood furniture, or hand-tailored clothes. But laziness and convenience will steer a lot of the writing and visual production towards the machines. For creative industries like advertising, the product we sell is attention. And attention is won with difference. Difference comes from associations like the ones described in this book—collisions between two previously unassociated ideas. But which ideas and in which way? That's likely to remain in the judgement of human

creative directors for a little while yet. Because if everyone has access to the standard solutions, the prize of attention won't be given to those using the same ideas as everyone else.

Guan: *Mashing up ideas doesn't come naturally. How can I train my brain to think that way?*
David: Our brains are hardwired to come up with familiar ideas. That's because we default to the familiar to save time and processing power in our system. We don't want to explore a hundred ways of putting on our socks each morning. But, of course, we may want to explore a hundred ways of selling a new brand of socks. And for the latter task, we need to address the fact that we have a different and less familiar task in front of us. One thing is to acknowledge the difficulty, and let your brain come up with all the familiar and done-before ideas first, just to get them out of your system. The question is how many ideas do you need to come up with before you have a decent solution? Well, a science fiction writer called Theodore Sturgeon might have accidentally hit on the answer. He was being interviewed by a sceptical journalist who said: 'Surely, 90 per cent of science fiction is crap.' and Sturgeon replied by saying, 'Well, 90 per cent of everything is crap.' And it seems to be true. In most competitions and prizes, around 10 per cent of entries are shortlisted. And in a list of top ten nominated movies, one is selected as 'best picture'. So that has given us a benchmark for saying that you probably need to come up with ten ideas to get one, and a hundred to get ten to choose from. In the age of AI, you probably need to push further than ever to get to unique and outstanding ideas.

Guan: *What's your favourite brainstorming technique to collide ideas?*
David: The best and most productive way to come up with ideas is to come up with as many as you can and write them down. It's important to write them out without judgement and without

inhibiting yourself by letting some inner voice criticize the quality of what you are doing. (If you are brainstorming in a group, don't let some outer voice criticize your fledgling ideas either!) It's also not a good idea to search the internet as you go—someone will almost certainly have done something like it but what you are doing isn't finished yet—so don't kill things too soon. The most important thing is to come back later and judge your ideas using logic. That's when you can unleash your inner critic and shoot down as many as you like. With luck, you'll be left with something after all is done.

Guan: *Thank you, David.*

David has shared some great reasons why we need to change our brains to be more creative. Humans are hardwired to solve problems using logic and accepted methods (just like AI). So to reach the ideas that AI can't, we need to think even more like humans. To get away from logic and embrace the illogical.

Imperfect Beauty

Before we learn how to change our brains, I should warn you about the biggest distraction to ideation—the urge to find perfection. While it seems like an admirable goal, it's actually a barrier to breakthrough thinking. The world we live in is not perfect. It's messy. And it's in this mess, that we find new ideas, new solutions and real connections.

I'd like to share a couple of stories with you before the training begins. The first one is a story from my life about the hunt for perfection. It's not pretty. But neither am I. As fate would have it, I was born with a cleft lip. So I learnt the hard way that the world was not perfect. At school, the kids were mean. They teased me. Called me 'clam mouth'. This damaged my self-esteem and made me think I was too ugly for anyone to love. But then I met my wife. We connected over a teddy bear that had been shared between our families. Miraculously, she saw past my physical imperfection, and we fell in love. On that day, I learnt an important lesson. Even if you think you're unattractive, someone will love you if you find the right connection.

After leaving school in Singapore, I moved to Los Angeles to study advertising. Every day, my lecturer would bark at me. He would drown the class in writing assignments. I'm not sure I ever once saw him smile. One day, I wrote something I was very proud of, and coming from Asia, I made sure the English was perfect. But when I got the assignment back, I was shocked to learn I had failed. How? Trembling in fear, I asked my lecturer why. He bluntly replied that my words sounded fake—as if written by robots. He said my words had no soul. He said that if I wanted to connect with humans, I had to humanize my writing with imperfections. Like using slang words or a conversational style.

In his own intimidating way, my lecturer had taught me an important lesson. That the 'perfect' words are the imperfect ones. And the 'perfect' ideas are imperfect too. Never run from imperfection—embrace it.

Wabi-sabi

Here's another quick tale about imperfection. In the Japanese language, they have a word called *'wabi-sabi'*. It's a noun that describes a way of life focused on finding beauty within imperfection. Peacefully accepting the natural cycle of growth and decay. I'm a huge fan of wabi-sabi. And I really enjoy saying the word out loud. Try it. It's fun.

This Japanese philosophy is a reminder of what makes ideas powerful. To work in the real world, ideas need to have the three Rs. They need to be relatable—showing familiar things or common ground. They need to be relevant—important to what your end user is concerned with. And they have to be real—building trust with honesty and authenticity.

Imperfection is not a handicap, but a natural part of life. To be embraced and celebrated, with inclusion and diversity. It is this imperfect beauty that helps us connect with other humans. In every endeavour in life, there is beauty in being real. Being authentic allows us to find connections with anyone.

In advertising for example, imperfect stories are told by many brands. One of the best examples of retail advertising I've ever seen was a film made by Volvo. Instead of hiring slick sales people to promote their cars, Volvo employed people who'd survived car crashes. It turns out they make incredible salespeople. After all, how many normal car salespeople can say: 'Let me show you the Volvo that saved my life.' But that's the pitch a real car crash survivor said to car shoppers in a campaign from New York agency, We Believers. During research, the agency discovered an important insight about car buyers. They discovered that car buyers tend to give priority to superficial features over safety, that is, until they've survived a serious crash.

The agency recruited a dozen car crash survivors, then got them to describe their accidents, and how being in a Volvo had saved their lives. One woman even showed prospective customers a copy of her X-rays. Another survivor said that at the scene of his accident, 'The paramedic said to the fireman that she was going to get a Volvo like mine.' While Volvo has long been known as a car with excellent safety features, this film delivered the idea of safety in a very real, powerful and imperfect way.[12]

I'll share with you one more example of imperfection that I believe is the best retail food commercial ever made. Have you ever seen photographs of McDonald's burgers or fries that are a few years old, and still look the same as the day they were bought? This is because they are full of artificial preservatives. Most processed foods are.

So when Burger King launched their new 'artificial-preservative-free' burgers in 2020, they decided to demonstrate the difference in a dramatic and imperfect way. Instead of showing a delicious-looking burger in their film like they normally do, they decided to show a decomposing whopper using time-lapse photography.

As you can imagine, the usual approach to filming burgers is to always show them in the best possible light. But the point of showing a decomposing burger was to show the burger contained no artificial preservatives. In the film, we see the burger starts off looking tasty, then it experiences the passage of time. The lettuce starts to wilt, the bun shrivels, and fuzzy white mould begins to cover the burger. After thirty-four days, the burger looked pretty gross. The message at the end of the film says, 'The beauty of real food is that it gets ugly. That's why we are rolling out a whopper that is free from artificial preservatives. Isn't it beautiful?' Burger King used imperfection to show people that natural burgers were better than unnatural burgers. And highlighted the benefit that real was better than fake. It was a master class in the beauty of imperfection.[13]

Those are just two examples of ideas that are relatable, relevant and real. And their authenticity is what makes these ideas so powerful. After you finish this book, and you begin to crash ideas together, remember to stay open to the imperfections in life. Instead of seeking the 'best idea ever', look for the idea that's relatable, relevant and real. Look for the imperfect idea that holds the strongest connection. And embrace the wabi-sabi.

If you're ready to begin, it's time to say goodbye to your old brain, and get ready to swap it with a new one. One that will make your ideas fresher, more unexpected and more potent than ever. I hope you're ready. Has the anaesthesia kicked in yet? If not, turn up the laughing gas, and pass me that rusty scalpel.

There is no such thing as a new idea. We simply take a lot of old ideas and put them into a sort of mental kaleidoscope.

Mark Twain (Samuel Clemens) [14]

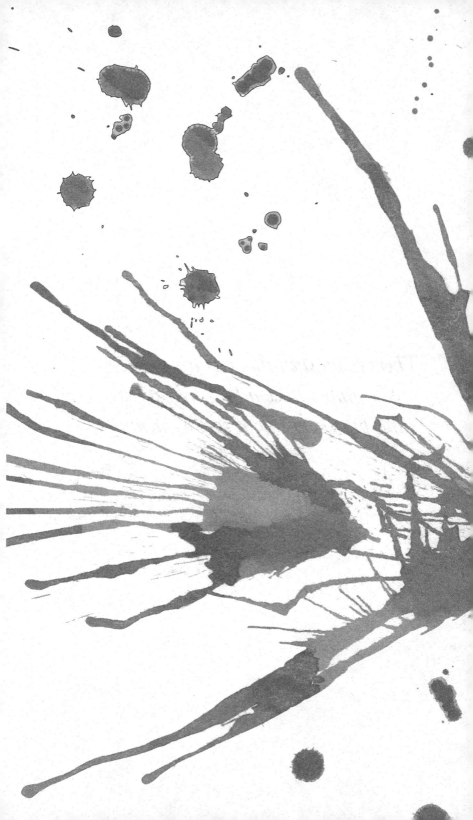

Chapter Five

CHAINSAW SURGERY FOR BEGINNERS

(Where I remove the gunk in your brain
using questionable methods).

Swap Your Brain For Mine

Right now you're probably thinking, *Sure, it's easy for you to come up with ideas, your brain probably works differently to mine.* That may be true, but I offer a simple, if slightly unnerving, solution to this dilemma.

What if your brain could be turned into mine? What if you could see the world the same way I do? Would that even be possible? It could be. But it's not painless. And you won't be the same person when it's over. Once you change the way your brain works, you will never look at the world the same way. You will gain a new way of thinking, but you will also lose the way you think now. That is the price you must pay. Do you still want to try? Then allow me to sterilize my scalpels and let's get started.

Before we can even think of coming up with ideas, the first step we need to do is change the way we think. As every child knows, you need to learn to walk before you can run. The same is true of creative ideation. Like an athlete, you need to prepare your mind to think in strange and lateral ways. It doesn't come naturally. And you'll always have the urge to revert to logical thinking. But thinking creatively can be learnt and mastered. By anyone, you included. We just need to crack open your brain, shove in the wonders of this world, scrape out the gunk and fire it up with the interconnectedness of everything.

Do you think you can handle that? In any case, we'll know soon, as this surgery is your first step on a perilous journey. The way forward is fraught with danger. And there's no guarantee you'll make it through alive. So take a deep breath. Hold my hand. And let's begin. Here are the techniques I use to help get my brain ready to collide.

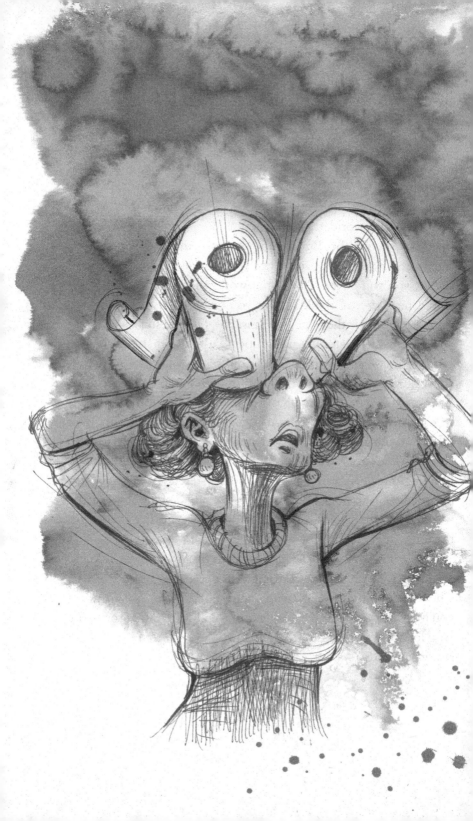

See Blindly

Observe life with an open mind. When you're trying to come up with ideas that make a difference in this world, you first need to know what the world really is. You need to understand why things are the way they are. How did we get here? Where do we go from here? What makes everything work? You must begin with an insatiable curiosity.

Sometimes we notice things without fully understanding or grasping their true meaning. In 2015, Bishop Gérald Caussé said, 'We look, but we don't really see; we hear, but we don't really listen.'[15] In my own life, I've been naïve, especially about relationships. Initially, I could only see the outer qualities of people I befriended. I didn't see their inner feelings, thoughts, or battles until it was too late. At times, this lack of understanding led to a relationship ending. Seeing blindly also means understanding and appreciating what you observe.

This shouldn't be done by sitting in front of a computer. This information is not something Google, Siri or Alexa can help you find. This is knowledge that must be learnt by experience. By observing other humans. Take time to notice patterns of behaviour. To find the things that motivate humans to action, you must learn the universal truths of humanity. Why do people do the things they do?

It doesn't matter what country you come from and what language you speak. Your race, age, gender and sexuality are also irrelevant. If you're a human, then you share universal traits with every other human.

On this planet, we all share the desire to give and receive love. And we all share the same fears and weaknesses too. To understand the world that surrounds us, you need to keep your eyes open and leave your judgement at home.

Once you learn to see blindly, you'll learn to see far.

Impossible Possibilities

School can be a wonderful experience. It gives us important knowledge like history, mathematics and science, while teaching us valuable skills like literacy, numeracy and communication. But this learning has a dark side effect. It teaches us to be logical, to follow the rules and abandon childish ways. By the time we become adults, many of us have lost touch with an ability we were all born with. The ability to believe.

We stop believing in fairies and dragons, we stop talking to imaginary friends and we stop believing in the impossible. This limits our sense of wonder, imagination and curiosity. Even worse, it hampers our lateral-thinking problem-solving abilities. If you don't believe in that which doesn't exist, how will you have any hope of creating it?

Being too logical is the same as being cynical. You can only see as far as the facts allow. This rarely, if ever, leads to new and powerful solutions to complex problems. But when you keep your mind open to impossible possibilities, you just might create one.

Now, for no reason whatsoever, here's an excerpt from a very old poem that captures the nonsensical, paradoxical nature of the impossible. I hope you like it.

TWO DEAD BOYS
One fine day, in the middle of the night
Two dead men, got up to fight
Back to back, they faced each other
Drew their swords and shot each other
A deaf policeman heard the noise
And came and killed those two dead boys
If you don't believe this lie is true
Ask the blind man, he saw it too
Unknown[16]

Try Everything

As humans, we always like to do predictable things. Things we are certain of, because we know the end result. This is comforting because it helps us maintain the illusion that we have some control over our circumstances. There is nothing wrong with being predictable, but it has a dire effect on solving problems. It tends to blunt our creative processes, and leads to boring solutions.

But fear not, brave adventurer, for we can break this pattern simply by trying new things. The more experiences you have, the more tools you will have to solve problems. Be unpredictable. Try different jobs. Start new hobbies. Travel the world. Eat exotic foods. Learn another language. Study philosophy. At the very least, change the way you walk to the bus stop each day. The more knowledge and wisdom you find, the easier it will be to find unpredictable solutions.

Yes, I realize this advice sounds like a clichéd motivational poster, but clichés usually become so because they are true. This is one of those times. To have strong ideation skills, we must put ourselves in the shoes of others, without prejudice. We must be armed with knowledge, understanding and real human insights.

Ralph Waldo Emerson once said, 'All life is an experiment. The more experiments you make, the better.'[17] I took this quote to heart and developed a never-ending thirst to embrace new experiences. I repaired tanks in Taiwan and tried sea walking in the coral islands of Thailand. I learnt how to ride a horse in Argentina and mastered the delicate brush strokes of Chinese painting. Every experience increased my lived-knowledge, and gave me tools I could use later in my creative endeavours.

And your experiences will too. Plus . . . trying new stuff is fun.

Find the Dots

I'm often asked, 'Where do you find your inspiration?' The boring answer is I try to learn as much about things as possible. Being inspired is easier when you have more knowledge.

I see myself as a detective, like Sherlock Holmes, seeking out the intricate web of connections that bind the facts before me. Holmes' way of seeing what goes unnoticed by others, keeping his judgement in check as he gathers information, and his unwavering focus on unearthing connections is a masterclass in problem-solving. Solving a mystery demands creativity, linking the unfamiliar, discovering hidden relations, and generating fresh perspectives from seemingly unrelated elements. Mental wandering paves the way for the unconscious mind to engage in what Einstein aptly named 'combinatory play'. This is the mind's unique way of marrying disparate ideas and influences, discovering fresh, new ways to fuse them.

A lot of people don't bother to do the research, and don't know what to join, so they make things up. But humans can't identify with ideas unless they're relevant. Finding the dots for your project is about researching and understanding everything about your project. You need to have enough material to be able to join the dots later. And the more you know, the better your choices will be. As British journalist Miles Kington once wrote, 'Knowledge is knowing that a tomato is a fruit. Wisdom is knowing not to put it in a fruit salad.' [18]

Finding an inspiring idea is not some kind of magic. It's a process that becomes automatic once you've crammed your brain with facts. You can't force it, but it comes naturally once you've programmed your brain with enough information to decide what to collide.

If you spend time finding the dots, you will build an unconscious collection of connections that will, later on, become obvious why they connect.

Which Clown Printed this Page Upside-down?

Not everything is as it appears. When you want to see things that aren't apparent, things that others can't see, a useful mindset to adopt is what I call upside-down thinking. Which simply means looking at things from every angle.

When people say 'think outside the box', what they really mean is, try to solve a problem using a fresh perspective. The first step is to ignore the accepted theory of how things should be done. There will be those who say, 'If it ain't broke, don't fix it.' But your job is to get away from this narrow, analytical thinking. Your job is to think beyond the boundaries. For new ideas to form, you must think without constraints. You must be free to challenge accepted wisdoms and turn them on their head.

A long time ago, I asked my copy partner James Scanlon to write a beer commercial celebrating the 2002 World Cup. I told him it *must* include scenes of football and drinking beer. He ignored me completely and forced himself to come up with ideas that had neither. The result? A multi-award-winning TV commercial that showed Europeans asleep at work because the World Cup was being played in Asia for the first time.

In your commercial or artistic endeavours, try to be a sceptic, without being a cynic. Sceptics ruthlessly seek the truth, while cynics believe everyone is motivated purely by self-interest. Are you motivated purely by self-interest? Or, as I suspect, are you motivated to make the world a better place?

If you are a true sceptic, then take the time to learn how things are done. Ask the important questions. Why are they done that way? What would you change to achieve a better result? Put yourself in the shoes of your customers. Not just the ones who like you, but the ones that dislike you too. What don't they like about your product? What do they like about your competitor's product? And while you're there, think like your competitors too. Ask yourself what does your worst enemy want you to do. Then, do the opposite.

In 2005, a Singaporean advertising agency called Eleven produced a highly innovative advertising campaign using this approach. Their creative director was my old friend James Scanlon. Eleven had been tasked with launching an American fast-food brand called Carl's Jr. into the Singapore market. But they faced an enormous problem. Their closest competitor, McDonald's, had a marketing budget of SGD $22 million. But Carl's Jr. budget was only SGD $220,000. How could they stand out with a budget that was literally 1 per cent of their competitor's?

The answer was to think sceptically. They knew that if they tried 'normal' ads, their messaging would be lost in the marketing noise created by McDonald's. Anything Carl's Jr. said could be said louder by the competition. So they came up with a very clever strategy. Do the opposite. Say the things that McDonald's couldn't say. Since McDonald's marketing was safe, clean, child-focused and 'healthy', the team at Eleven decided the marketing for Carl's Jr. would be dangerous, messy, adult-oriented and honest. Brutally honest.

As we all know, burgers are junk food. But it's very rare to find someone in marketing prepared to admit it. That is, until Carl's Jr. and Eleven were courageous enough to try. Together, they came up with ads that screamed unhealthy. They exposed the dangerous outcomes of eating burgers, both social and physical, using headlines such as, 'Not recommended by doctors', 'Parental guidance advised' and 'Screw the diet'.

This refreshingly honest approach resonated with Singaporeans, and gave the brand a lot of street credibility. It instantly became the 'cool' junk food brand. The launch was an outstanding success, establishing four stores in the first year and achieving sales transactions 45 per cent higher than projected targets. The campaign went on to win the top award in Singapore for marketing effectiveness (a Gold Effie), and the strategy and slogan (It's gonna get messy.) were used for an additional fifteen years to launch the brand in seven additional countries.

This is an outstanding example of thinking outside the box by challenging accepted wisdoms to find fresh perspectives. It demonstrates that looking at problems from every angle lets you discover new viewpoints not available with straightforward analysis. And it shows that even tiny budgets can deliver big results, because fortune favours the bold.

If you're looking for a fresh solution, think outside accepted norms.

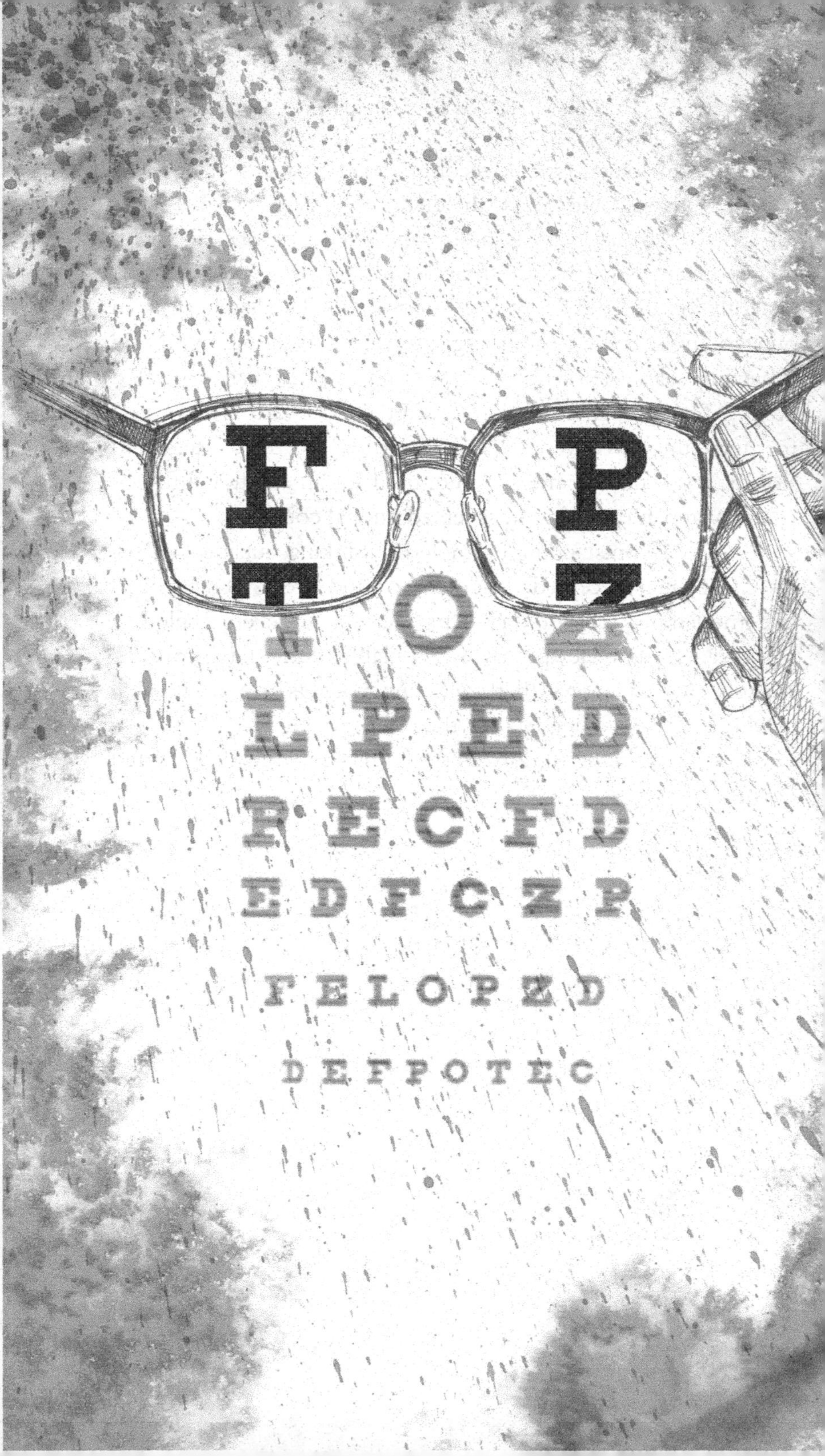
F P
T O Z
L P E D
P E C F D
E D F C Z P
F E L O P Z D
D E F P O T E C

Noise, Smoke and Bubbles

In the last twenty-five years, the Internet has changed the world in a multitude of profound ways. It has changed every part of the globe. It has changed us economically, socially and politically. The Internet has literally changed the way we do everything. Personally, I'm a huge fan. But it comes at a steep price.

We now live in a cloud of misinformation that surrounds, and envelops us all. We all exist in our own bubble of opinions, misconceptions and urban myths. For instance, some people believe the myth that Australia is dangerous because of deadly animals like snakes, spiders and crocodiles. More on that myth shortly.

You see, the problem with living in our own bespoke bubble, surrounded by a cloud of dodgy information, is it takes away our ability to see clearly. It limits our ability to find connections that are real. And we lose the ability to understand our fellow humans. Ultimately, we lose our ability to connect.

Soren Kierkegaard was a famous Danish theologian and existentialist philosopher in the nineteenth century. He offered a very astute observation about the truth. In English translations of his original Dutch writings, he says: 'There are two ways to be fooled. One is to believe what isn't true; the other is to refuse to believe what is true.' If you meet someone who is a conspiracy theorist and believes the moon landing was faked, or the earth is flat, you'll understand they have allowed themselves to be fooled both ways. And that's why they have lost the ability to connect with their fellow humans who aren't fooled by conspiracy theories.

Another great quote is from the Roman emperor Marcus Aurelius Antoninus. He said: 'Everything we hear is an opinion, not a fact. Everything we see is a perspective, not the truth.' This is a profound thought about how opinion and perspective are not facts. It's also a great example of misinformation. Because the truth is . . . the emperor never said it.

As it happens, there were two Roman emperors called Marcus Aurelius Antoninus. One was emperor from 161 to 180 AD and a Stoic philosopher. The other Marcus Aurelius Antoninus (nicknamed Caracalla), was emperor from 198 to 217 AD. And this quote was never said by either of these two men.

The quote actually comes from a 2019 post on an Instagram account called @jimcarreyhere. (Note: whoever runs this account is *not* the actor Jim Carrey. The real Jim Carrey has his own official Twitter account). Instead, this quote has been made up by some anonymous person and attributed to Marcus Aurelius Antoninus. I just like it because it's a great example of how easily we can be fooled by fake information when it sounds true.

So what can we do to ensure we have a clear understanding of the world around us? Learn from people who know the truth. Listen to experts, not some guy with a blog. We can study at universities and read books. And we can steer clear of trying to source facts (or quotes) from the internet.

Whenever I have a subjective opinion about something, I seek out the views of someone who has the opposite subjective opinion. Then I try to understand why. After all, most humans are good-hearted people trying to make the world a better place. They just approach it from different angles. Once I understand their reasoning, it always leads me to a more objective opinion. And a truer understanding of 'the truth'.

Another way to fix this is to ignore the sensationalist clickbait of life. To take the time to disengage from social echo chambers and look for real human truths. To turn off the noise of fake news, see through the smoke of post-truth propaganda and pop your own bubble of confirmation bias. If you manage to learn how to see past the noise, smoke and bubbles, please teach me how to do it.

If you can't differentiate between what is real and what is fake, you will never connect with people. It will seriously limit your ability to find connections that are real. Speaking of reality, let's get back to the myth that Australia is dangerous because of all the venomous snakes and spiders, and hungry, hungry crocodiles. This myth is dangerous because it teaches us to fear things that, in all likelihood, won't kill us. And makes us feel safe around the actual animals that will kill us. So if you'd like a brief glimpse of life outside the matrix, the next page shows you Australia's most dangerous animal.

The real one.

Are You Terrified Yet? You Should Be

In Australia, horses, cows and dogs cause 50 per cent of animal-related deaths. Horses alone kill more people than sharks, crocodiles, spiders and snakes combined. Beware the horse.[19]

Think Laterally

Where do creative people get their crazy ideas? Are they born with it? Does a supernatural muse send them ideas? Or maybe their brains were altered during a traumatic childhood? As it happens, I don't get my inspiration from any of these sources. But I have learnt there's a way to come up with new ideas, without relying on luck, ghosts or tragedy. It's called Lateral Thinking.

Made famous in 1967 by Maltese psychologist Edward de Bono, lateral thinking is a way of thinking that helps us solve problems using an indirect approach, with reasoning that is not immediately obvious. The way we normally think is called Critical Thinking, where we use logical analysis to judge the true value of statements. Our brains will follow well-worn pathways to reach conclusions we know have worked before. This is a logical and rational way of thinking, and serves us well in most situations. Except when we are trying to come up with new ideas, because Critical Thinking only takes us to places in our brain we've already been.

Lateral Thinking, however, shows us how to move our thinking from known solutions to unknown solutions. It teaches us how to reach the parts of our brain we've never been to. And how to create random pathways that lead to new ideas. Thinking laterally is like supercharging your brain, or giving it an upgrade. It's an incredibly strong tool for ideation, and a way of reaching ideas we never knew existed.

Here's an example of how a team I led used lateral thinking to solve a problem. At Leo Burnett, my team was trying to come up with ideas for an ultra-bright light bulb. They initially focused on presenting the bulbs as the product. Showing the level of brightness, talking about positive uses for bright lights, and showing the technology behind the brightness. While these were all very 'worthy' ideas from an engineer's perspective, from an advertising perspective they were all overly logical, and yawn-worthy solutions.

The team knew they couldn't bore people into buying the product. They knew that if the idea to sell the bulbs wasn't interesting, customers wouldn't even notice the ad in the first place.

So we introduced a provocation. This is an idea that moves thinking forward to a new place where new ideas can be found. We asked the question, 'What are the bad things that happen when you don't have bright light?' You could bump into furniture in the dark. You could get mugged in a dark alley. Ships would crash on the rocks without a bright lighthouse. And children would be scared of the dark. We tried another provocation. 'Why are children scared of the dark?' Answer: Because there are monsters hiding in the closet and under the bed.

We were getting closer, but the creative solutions were only showing non-scared children in bright rooms. Still boring. So we tried one more provocation. 'If the monsters go away from bright lights, where do they go?' They go somewhere else. In effect, they become homeless. And just like that, we had an intriguing insight—bright lights make monsters homeless. All that remained was to find an execution.

We tried lots of different ways to show this idea, until we finally developed a creative campaign showing photos of scary monsters living rough on the streets, because ultra-bright light bulbs had driven them from their hiding spots, rendering them homeless. The slogan was, 'Banish monsters from under the bed.' It was an unexpected and award-winning solution that was born using lateral thinking.

Since the techniques and methods behind lateral thinking are not mine, I think it's best to learn it straight from the person who invented it. On the next page are some books about lateral thinking written by Edward De Bono. They can be quite dense to read, but stick with them, because lateral thinking is an extremely valuable ideation skill that's worth learning. And these books contain great techniques and examples you can follow.

Lateral Thinking

This is the book that started the lateral thinking revolution. It's probably the most important book in the world for teaching creative thinking.

How To Have Creative Ideas

Reading this book is like having a personal trainer for your brain. It teaches you sixty-two games and exercises you can use to train your brain to think creatively.

Six Thinking Hats

This book shows you how to investigate an idea from six different angles using a lateral technique called parallel thinking. This makes you more efficient and more productive.

Without lifting your pencil, draw four straight lines that connect all the dots. The answer is at the end of the book.

Genius Thinking

Do you always think of average ideas? Maybe you've been filling your mind with garbage. Maybe you've been watching reality TV or some other junk food for the mind. Don't worry. There's an easy solution to that problem. Just stop looking at garbage.

To think like a genius, you should learn from genius thinkers. Copy their ways and use their thinking as your benchmark. Experience the world's best films, music, art and literature. Look at award-winning websites, podcasts, influencers and social media. This trains your brain to think big and to recognize greatness.

And you shouldn't confine yourself to artistic leaders. Study philosophical giants as well. Like Aristotle, Socrates and Plato. And Lao Tzu, Buddha and Confucius. The more you understand how humanity works, the more resonant your ideas will become.

When searching for a top art school in America, my Uncle Gaw Sin Hock, suggested the ArtCenter College of Design in Pasadena. He said, 'If you want to succeed in the advertising business, you need to study in a school taught by the best creative leaders in the industry, and not teachers. It's the network that will take you far and not your degree.' This sage advice served me well.

In your professional life, seek out the award-winners in your industry. What did they do that was different to everyone else? It's simple really. Once your mind is filled with groundbreaking solutions, your brain will become an expert at recognizing a great idea.

To be a genius, you must think like a genius.

If I have seen further, it is by standing on the shoulders of giants.
Isaac Newton [20]

Learn to Juggle

I don't mean the kind of juggling with balls and flaming batons (unless you'd like a career in the circus). I mean multitasking. Personally, I like to work on half a dozen projects at the same time. This helps me to get stronger ideas, faster. Let me explain how it works.

When trying to come up with ideas, there will be moments when you get stuck. When the problem you are trying to solve seems impossible. You may feel like you've reached a dead end. This is a common occurrence in ideation. And if you only work on one project at a time, this will slow you down considerably. Having multiple projects open at the same time allows you to jump from one problem to another.

So if you're stuck trying to come with an idea, you can switch topics and change the context. In my experience, inspiration often strikes when you take an idea from its original context and move it somewhere else. It gives your mind space to let the previous problem percolate in your subconscious. More often than not—almost like magic—a solution will pop into your mind. And even if it doesn't, you'll return to the previous project with a refreshed perspective.

In my professional life, I am employed in an advertising agency. Working with multiple brands in an agency setting is something I genuinely enjoy. It facilitates the exchange of insights from one project to the next and keeps things interesting as I navigate diverse problems.

Working on multiple projects simultaneously is an easy way to improve your creative thinking. You'll work much faster and find better solutions. Multitasking makes you more creative by making you more productive.

Ordinary Beauty

Finding inspiration comes easiest to the curious mind. When you actively look for beauty in the everyday, you'll change the way your brain works. You will gain the superpower of being able to find solutions, like a truffle-sniffing pig.

Inspiration is all around us. There is beauty everywhere, in everything. You can find it in the natural world as easily as you can find it in an urban environment. It's especially visible in the human experience. All you need to do is be ready to see it. If you're feeling uninspired, you probably haven't opened your eyes to the world.

Look for the beauty hidden in seemingly insignificant parts of our daily routine. Not just the triumphs and celebrations, but in the everyday struggles and tragedies. See the beauty in small glances and nuanced reactions.

From the natural world to human-made objects, small moments of profound wonderment are easy to find. There is even beauty in pollution. Have you ever seen the rainbow colours formed on the surface of an oil slick? When you see sublime beauty in something so intrinsically ugly, it always provokes new ways of thinking.

Every day, I tell myself to stop and see the colourful world around me. Life isn't just wonderful during significant events; it's also full of wonder in the smallest of moments. There is a quiet beauty in the strength people show every day. And small gestures can mean a lot. I work hard to make sure I notice how amazing life is, even in the smallest of moments. By doing this, I feel more inspired to take on what is ahead.

So wherever you are, remember to open your eyes, ears and heart. If you look for the ordinary beauty that surrounds us, it won't take you long to find inspiration.

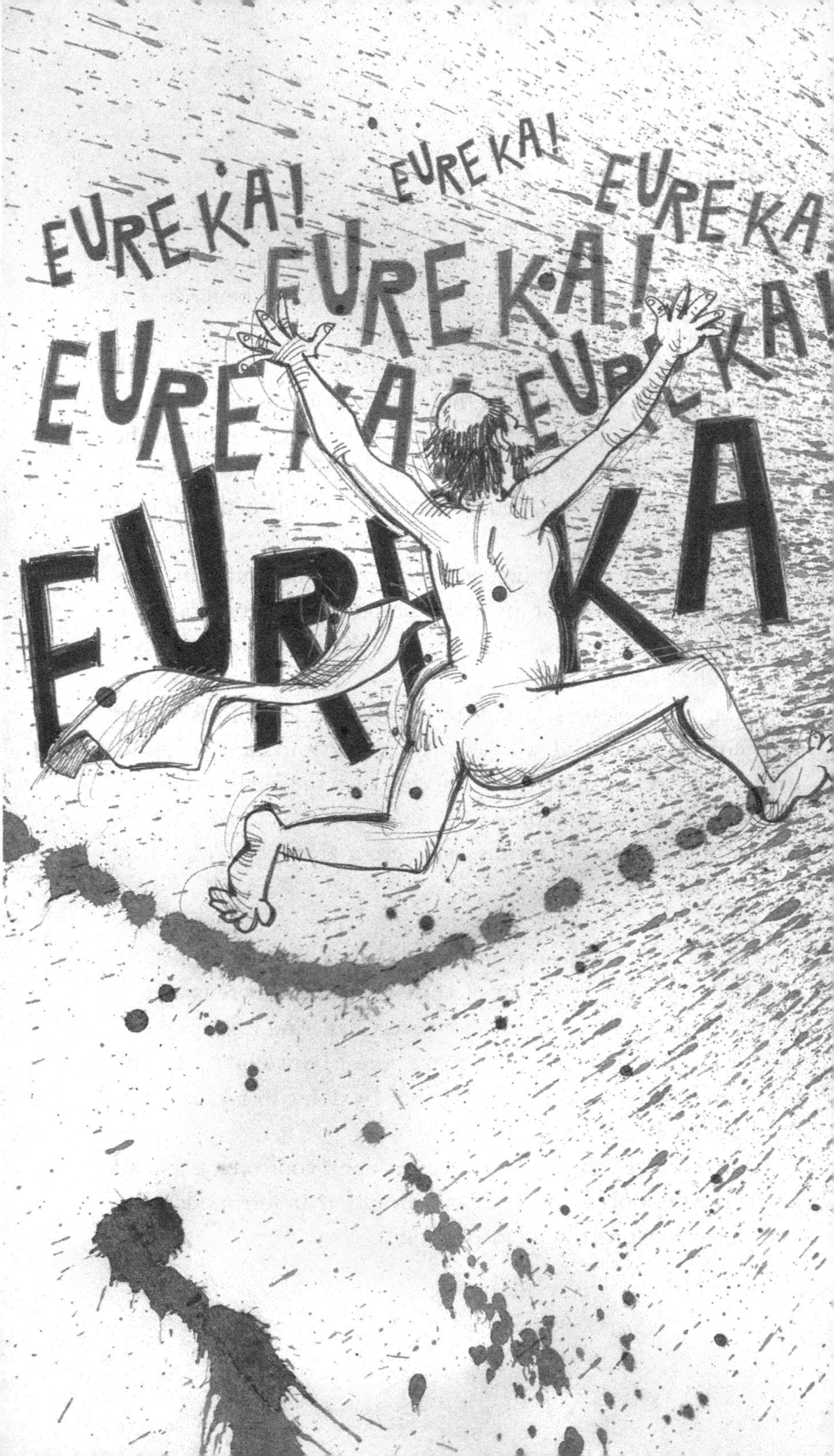
EUREKA!
EUREKA!
EUREKA
EUREKA!
EUREKA

Thrilling Boredom

Smartphones offer fun ways to waste time. Whenever I'm on the bus, or waiting for the kettle to boil, I'm always tempted to watch a TikTok, scroll through my socials or play some Candy Crush. How did we live before these wonderful toys were invented? The short answer is—we got bored.

But boredom is not a waste of time. In fact, the opposite is true. Boredom offers a great benefit. It allows our minds to wander. To think of random things. To play mental games with ourselves. Before smartphones were invented, we would fill this boredom with daydreaming—one of the key ingredients for imagination. We would drift away in thought, and imagine what it would be like to be a pirate. And then, during some idle moment while folding laundry, a brilliant solution to another problem would jump up and smack us in the face. And that is the importance of mental boredom. To allow the 'Eureka!' moment. Rather than being a time sink, daydreaming is a source of creative inspiration.

Claire Zedelius is an assistant project scientist in the Psychological and Brain Sciences department at the University of California, Santa Barbara. She earned her PhD in social psychology from Utrecht University in the Netherlands. Her research focuses on mind wandering, creativity and curiosity. Together with fellow researchers, she conducted pilot studies, asking online participants to recall their most recent daydreams. They identified six underlying dimensions that capture distinct qualities of daydreams. These were: how pleasant (or unpleasant) a daydream is, how much it revolves around mundane planning, how much it involves sexual thoughts, whether it is deliberate or unconscious, how personally meaningful it is, and how fantastical it is. Any one daydream can include any or all of these six qualities. Participants who found their daydreams meaningful reported greater inspiration at the end of the day, and those who frequently reported fantastical daydreams reported more creative behaviour.[21]

There are many distractions to daydreaming that come and go. But digital technology is a constant distraction. When your brain is always in a highly active mode, it can prevent you from focusing on deeper thinking. Even when we are not using our smartphones, they call to us in seductive dings, stopping us from daydreaming.

These devices are stealing your best ideas. The ones you get when you least expect it. If you want your creativity to increase dramatically, spend less time on your phone, and more time staring out the window. Try baby steps first. Switch your phone off for one hour every day while you catch public transport or do some chores at home. Easier said than done, I know, but worth a try for the immediate benefits to your thought processing.

Whenever I switch my phone off, I notice an immediate benefit to my brain's ability to have an idea. After letting things sit, insights come up from the deeper layers of my mind and break into my conscious awareness, often dramatically. The sudden 'Eureka!' moments happen when I'm in the shower, walking, or busy with something unrelated. The solution just pops up, seemingly out of nowhere.

Speaking of showers, another technique I use to complement boredom is the frequent application of negative ions. Right now, I'm sure you're thinking *What kind of hippy nonsense is this?* Well, it's nonsense backed by many scientific studies, including ones done by Columbia University in New York. Breathing in negative ions is believed to produce biochemical reactions that increase levels of serotonin, helping to alleviate depression, relieve stress and boost mental energy.[22]

Negative ions are created as air molecules break apart due to sunlight, radiation and, most importantly, crashing water.

It was Nobel Prize-winning German physicist Philipp Eduard Anton Lenard who discovered that air tends to be more negatively charged when water splashes.[23] For me, I like to get my daily dose by sitting at a beach with crashing waves, or next to a raging river or waterfall. If I can't get access to those sources, I simply turn on a hot, steamy shower and stand under it for ten minutes.

If you live in a desert, or don't have access to running water, you can invest in a cheap negative ion generator that is the size of a deck of cards. Called ionisers, these devices are available online and at most electronics stores. Stick one on your desk at work and spend your days getting bathed in these odourless, tasteless molecules. Combine it with a little boredom, and watch your brain's creativity increase.

Wash Your Brain

The brain surgery is almost complete. But before you begin colliding ideas, there's one last thing you need to do. It's called brainwashing. Not the bad kind done by politicians, cults and dodgy sales people. It's the good kind where you clean your brain.

We all carry worries with us. Some exist at a conscious level. Some are deep in the subconscious. Either way, they take up space in our brain, distracting us from focusing on things. These worries range from the banal to the serious. But mostly, they are everyday worries, like the rent is late, or that mole on your nose is getting bigger.

Whatever worries you have, they are clogging up valuable brain space and you have to get rid of them. For me, I like to begin each day with a five-minute meditation. I find it's the fastest, easiest way to add additional clarity and focus to my thinking. It gets rid of all the trash on my mental desktop. And helps me begin creative collisions with a fresh, lemon-scented brain.

Now, if you're not a great believer in meditation techniques, then you could try taking a 'time out'. You could take a walk outside, sit under a tree, or whack your headphones on and blast out a banger. It really doesn't matter what you do, as long as you give your brain a moment of peace. A short break from the constant storm of worries clouding our brains.

If you are willing to consider meditation but, maybe, it didn't work for you in the past, open up Google and search for websites that provide free, brief meditation techniques. You'll find plenty to try.

Okay Guan, I Tried Meditating and it Didn't Work

Fret not, my friend, this often happens with intelligent people like you and me. For some of us, meditating can be extremely hard. Our brains are too full of noisy thoughts to calm down. And sometimes our brains absorb too much fake information and it clouds our thinking. So if washing your brain with a five-minute meditation isn't working, it's time for what I call a 'deep clean'.

As we pass through life, negative thoughts can build up like dust in a carpet, until our brain looks like a filthy, abandoned house, instead of a shiny new condo. That's when I know it's time to deep-clean my mind, removing outdated thoughts and mending broken thought processes. Sometimes beneficial mindfulness practices like meditation and yoga just aren't enough. Sometimes, it feels necessary to undergo a significant mental refresh, akin to a professional house deep cleaning.

Sadly, I haven't come across any professional brain-cleaning service yet. So I've created my own methods of decluttering and refreshing my mind. These seven strategies shown below will benefit anyone who feels similarly overwhelmed and could use their own mental spring clean.

1. Before jumping into my task list, I take five minutes to count my breaths. This is like counting sheep to fall asleep, except I do it to calm my brain. Focusing on breathing and counting at the same time is very calming. And when I re-emerge from this little exercise, I find my focus has become razor-sharp.

2. I also like to concentrate on environmental sensations and sounds. This allows my mind to melt into the present. I close my eyes and listen. How many distinct sounds can I hear? How many sensations can I feel?

3. To deepen my experience of being mindful. I often consume food and drinks with my eyes closed. This allows me to explore each flavour and texture sensation with my taste buds. And when I close my eyes to eat, food tastes better too.

4. I also like the refreshing quality of walking meditation. Who says you need to sit in the lotus position to meditate? I take a stroll through nature and visualize myself being one with nature. What would it be like to be a tree? A leaf? An ant?

5. Repeating a silent mantra also helps me clear my mind. A commonly practised mantra is *OM MANI PADME HUM* from Buddhism. But I like to use *OOGA-CHAKA*, the chant used in the song 'Hooked on a feeling'. Simply because it makes me smile.

6. Sometimes I try a visualization-based meditation. This is like making a movie in your head. For example, imagine you're an astronaut going to Mars. Visualize the training. Watch the blast-off and long journey. See the landing. Explore Mars. But don't get eaten by the Martians.

7. My last strategy is to take my dog for a long walk. If you don't have one, offer to walk your neighbour's. Watch how the dog sees the world. Imagine you're the dog. Feel its unabashed excitement at spontaneous moments like sniffing butts and peeing on trees. Life becomes simple when you think like a dog.

Playtime is Never Over

There are many games I play that bolster my cognitive abilities. Beyond just entertainment, playing games requires me to process and manipulate information in various forms. This enhances my memory, attention span, spatial reasoning and mental flexibility. Of course, there are many adults who believe games are just for kids. For your sake, I hope you're not one of them. If you are, then put this book down right now and get out and play a game. *(Have they left yet? Okay, the rest of us can continue).*

Puzzle games, for instance, stimulate my logical thinking and pattern-recognition abilities. They present an intellectual challenge, a problem that must be solved by navigating the abstract mazes woven by the designers. Each puzzle solved is a testament to my growing mental acuity and refined critical thinking.

When I play hide-and-seek with my kids, it forces me to look beyond the obvious, and see things that aren't there. It teaches me to analyse the environment and find hidden clues. Looking at a *Where's Wally?* book does the same thing. For those who have been living under a rock, *Where's Wally?* is a series of search-and-find books created by British illustrator Martin Handford.[24] There are sixteen books in total, published in thirty-one languages. Here's a fun fact. Did you know he's not called Wally in every country? In the US and Canada, his name is Waldo. In Denmark, he is known as Holger. In France, his name is Charlie. And in Germany, they call him Walter.

When I'm out playing Paintball, I tap into my old army training and start to devise strategic ways to win against opponents. This gives me great strategic skills to solve other problems. Chess is a great game for improving strategic thinking as well.

For problem solving, I like to work on brainteasers in the form of riddles. These act as fun, mental exercises that improve logic, lateral thinking and memory skills at the same time.

Here's one for you. 'A woman pushes her car to a hotel, and tells the owner she's bankrupt. Why?' The answer is at the bottom of this page.

Role-playing games like Red Dead Redemption work differently, but equally significantly. They bolster my imagination and storytelling skills, allowing me to delve into fictional universes and adopt the roles of diverse characters. My understanding of the narrative structure and character development deepens through each storyline, plot twist and character interaction. Plus, I just like robbing trains!

I don't just see games as mere entertainment. I see games are a conduit for my creativity, exposing me to new and diverse scenarios, characters and mechanics. Each unique experience inspires me, sparks my ideas and encourages me to envision new concepts. In essence, games are creative tools. They are an interactive canvas where I can observe, learn and adapt.

So stop being such an adult, and get out and play some games. You'll have lots of fun, and become more creative in the process.

Answer: She's playing Monopoly.

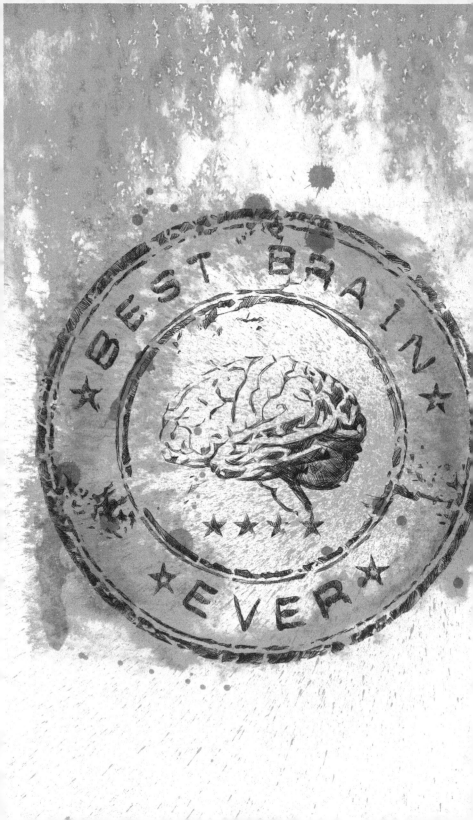

Welcome to Your Upgraded Brain

Was the brain transplant successful? Are you feeling okay? Hopefully, that wasn't too painful. Can you remember your name? Do you know today's date? If so, we can proceed.

If the operation was a success, and your body hasn't rejected your new brain, then you'll notice a few changes. You'll notice improvements in the way you think, as you start to think laterally outside the box. You'll notice you've got a handle on the zeitgeist and are able to see the world clearly. You'll actively seek out new experiences, appreciate the beauty in the everyday and understand the importance of boredom. You believe in the impossible. Your brain is making new connections as you look at things from different angles, and you now feel at ease juggling multiple problems at once. You've washed your brain and you're ready to play.

Congratulations! The first part of our perilous journey is complete. If you can still read this, and you're not drooling vacantly, it means you've successfully swapped your brain for mine. We've just dropped nitrous oxide into your brain's combustion chamber and added a serious amount of horsepower to your thought engine. I'm sure you are keen to take your new turbo brain out for a test drive. But first we must prepare a safe place for ideation. We don't want there to be any accidents like last time.

Make sure you're sitting down, your seatbelt is securely fastened and let's get to the safety presentation in the next chapter.

Creativity is inventing, experimenting, growing, taking risks, breaking rules, making mistakes and having fun.

Mary Lou Cook [25]

Interview with **KOREAN GIANT** Thomas Hong-tack Kim

Before we head to the next chapter, which is all about colliding safely with others, let's take a short break and hear from one of South Korea's most awarded creative directors. Thomas Hong-tack Kim is currently the chief creative officer at Paulus, and has spent over thirty years in the advertising industry. Most notably twenty years at Cheil Worldwide, where he was an executive creative director of the agency's Creative Innovation Group.

On top of his many advertising awards, Kim is a prominent ad critic in Korea and author of six books on advertising and culture. Since 2016, Hong-tack has been a creative solutionist and founder of '2kg', Creative Solution Lab and a visiting professor of Yonsei University.

Guan: *Hi Hong-tack, you're probably the most famous Korean person in advertising. How would you describe the process of creative conflict?*
Hong-tack: I would say creative conflict is like a chemical reaction of sources to create a totally new world, rather than a physical bond of sources.

Guan: *That's a philosophical way of saying it. Tell me, how important is it to create a culture of collaboration within a company?*
Hong-tack: Developing concepts together based on the 'why' is the most important thing. If you get that right, the 'what' and the 'how' are relatively easy. After that, it's also important to collaborate and share around your respective areas of expertise.

Guan: *What are the dangers in collaboration? Are there opportunities in the new way of collaborating in today's world?*
Hong-tack: The presence of modulators is important. In the past, when we were handling traditional media, the role of the

creative director was very important. They direct everything. It's collaboration, but it's vertical collaboration. Today, in a horizontal collaboration like we have now, where everyone's expertise is very different, you need to recognize each other's expertise and try to build consensus. The creative director's role should also shift from giving direction to focusing on coordination.

Guan: *One of the topics I write about in this book is how robots are taking over our jobs. What creative skills do humans need to remain relevant?*
Hong-tack: Artificial Intelligence has the net capability to take over simple but time-consuming processes that humans used to do, such as data gathering and analysis outlines. In doing so, AI can deliver optimized results that humans need. Human intelligence, on the other hand, is about finding insights and creating solutions based on them. It needs to be trained on what insights to look for in the data.

Guan: *Many things are driven by data these days. Can it be used creatively? How can data analysis help the mash-up process of ideation?*
Hong-tack: If you're not getting insights from your data, it's just a bunch of data junk. Insights are very important, especially in commercial communications. After analysing the data to find meaningful insights that are specific to each project, a mash-up process based on those insights will yield very rich results.

Guan: *Cool. What's your favourite brainstorming technique to collide ideas?*
Hong-tack: Write keywords from your ideas on post-it notes and categorize them into similar themes or characters. It's like drawing a mental map of sorts. You'll find commonalities. Even if your thoughts are different from each other, you can find a common thread of insights. Use those insights to find solutions.

Guan: *Once you think you've solved a problem using creative conflict, how do you know when you've found a working solution?*

Hong-tack: The first thing to consider is whether the solution is in the right direction. Next, you should consider whether the solution is easily understood and unique.

Guan: *One last question. What advice would you give to help someone learning about creative conflict?*

Hong-tack: Conflict is inevitable in creative work. If the conflict is bigger than you think, take a step back, pause, and revisit your ideas or opinions the next day. It's an exercise in taking an objective view of your idea. This will help you to see its flaws and how you can improve it. In the end, it will be much easier to take the right direction.

Guan: *Gam-sa-ham-ni-da* (Thank you), *Hong-tack, for your wise advice.*

There is a very useful insight in this interview about a new way of working called horizontal collaboration. Instead of directing the process from the top down (vertical collaboration), a more effective way is to utilize everyone's expertise in a brainstorming session to reach a consensus amongst participants.

This is easier said than done, so in the next chapter I will show you how to do it safely.

Chapter Six

FOR MAX CARNAGE USE BUBBLE WRAP

(Where I share dubious safety tips on
how to break stuff with humans).

Colliding With Others

There should be a signpost here that says, *Warning. Danger Ahead.* Because you're about to learn how to smash your new brain into other brains, and colliding with others is filled with many dangerous obstacles.

Are the hairs on your neck standing up? They should be. Maybe your palms are getting a little sweaty just thinking about brainstorming with others. Fear not, for I will have a tight grip on your clammy hand throughout this whole chapter.

Fear of conflict is real, but fear is also an illusion. If you don't understand how to make brainstorming safe, you will naturally fear it will lead to unproductive conflict and failure. But once you understand how to build a kind, gentle open space, your fears will disappear as you realize conflict can be a positive, productive tool.

Those who use creative conflict wisely have no fear. They know that when properly managed, conflict leads to powerful solutions. And they know it needs to be done right. Creative conflict is too powerful to be released unsupervised into a group. Colliding with others needs to be a managed experience. Once you have the right culture and environment, someone needs to direct the process. You need to select the right people and brief them correctly. And you need to give them freedom and the right tools.

Once you adopt the following skills and techniques, you will be able to foster creative conflict efficiently and unleash the potential of your team. When you have effective collaboration, you will harness diverse perspectives to find truly innovative ideas, instead of the obvious ones. Obviously.

Here are some important things you need to consider.

A Dangerously Safe Space

Before smashing our heads together like rutting goats, it's important to have a safe space. One where there are clear objectives and the parameters are known. One where the participants feel safe to say whatever is on their mind, free of filters. If there are any constraints on thinking, your brainstorming will only reveal ideas that are complacent, mediocre and designed to maintain the status quo.

To do it successfully begins with your company's culture. Has management made innovation a driving purpose? This is very important. Do you have an agreement on how creative conflict will be used to drive innovation? Is there an implementation process in place? Has the company established the cultural conditions that teams need to thrive? What methodology will be used to collide productively?

There are many things to consider when creating a brainstorming environment that is productive and profitable. But having the right culture in a company, with open minds and safe spaces, means people can collaborate without their egos coming into play. This leads to useful and productive creative conflict.

But be warned, without the right culture, this conflict can lead to inefficient thinking. This will generate ideas that cannot be implemented. There will be fierce competition amongst staff and feelings will be hurt. Lastly, you will create an unnecessary drag on quality and productivity. And trust me, nobody wants that.

But if you take the time to prepare a carefully considered environment in which to brainstorm, you will turn the innovation process into a highly efficient, productive and profitable exercise. And everybody wants that.

That's All Well and Good, But Can You Give Me an Example

I sure can. I'm glad you asked. At an advertising agency called J. Walter Thompson, the usual way to brainstorm was to find an empty room and try to think of ideas. But sitting in these void spaces was very unstimulating. The people tasked with coming up with new ideas often felt constrained in their thinking. And it showed in their ideas which were stale, boring, expected and obvious. Something had to be done to break this sterile environment.

So I challenged the status quo and injected a thrilling twist into our typical brainstorming routine. Instead of marinating in the same stale office surroundings, I proposed a plan to my agency team: to carve out an entirely new creative space. One that had never been used before.

Our mission? To come up with new ideas for a unique perfume soap variant. Our venue? Nothing less than a sprawling, opulent hotel suite, commandeered entirely for our cause. *(Please excuse the overuse of adjectives in the next few paragraphs, but I'd like to give you a hyperbolic taste of the experience).*

We began first by transforming every corner of the suite into a showcase of our products, changing the numerous bathrooms into experimental hotspots. All workshop participants were plunged into an immersive, hands-on experience, directly interacting with the products in their destined habitat.

But we didn't stop there. We escalated the atmosphere to another sensory level. We enlisted the expertise of real, seasoned perfumers who meticulously crafted an extravagant sensory realm for us. Different themed rooms sprung to life, each one stimulating the senses, invoking inspiration and excitement at every turn. The participants were transported to a fantastical world of scents and sensory experiences. And the entire event was an unforgettable spectacle, an explosion of innovation.

The new concepts that emerged from this adrenaline-infused brainstorming were groundbreaking. A thrilling mix of innovation and excitement that had never been seen before. This wasn't just a meeting; it was a sensory revolution, forever transforming how we approached creativity and concept generation. And it wasn't just a dangerously safe space. It was a completely new space that stimulated completely new ideas. *(Okay, I'll cut down on the overuse of adjectives now)*.

The simple fact that we changed a sterile environment into a sensory one was all it took to change sterile ideas into fresh ideas. And if that's what we did to come up with new ideas for a soap brand, imagine what kind of environment you can create in your business for something more meaningful.

Creating the right space also works when presenting ideas. A friend of mine in Hong Kong was pitching to get the job to design the Shell Shops attached to service stations. Normally, this involved creating a PowerPoint document with lots of illustrations showing the new design. Instead, they transformed their boardroom into an actual Shell Shop, complete with shelves, products, cash registers, employees and uniforms. Instead of a boring presentation, they welcomed the client with just six words: 'Welcome to your new Shell Shop'. The client could interact in a real three-dimensional space, touching things and getting a tactile demonstration that couldn't be found in a dry PowerPoint. Needless to say, my friend won the business.

The Right Wrong People

In your company, who are the right people to do the ideation? Is it the bosses, since they make the final decisions? Or is it the 'creative types' who are trained for this sort of thing? Who is the right person for ideation? The good news is, you are.

That's right. There's no one out there with a monopoly on creative thinking. We all have it within us, as long as the conditions are right. As long as we are the right kind of wrong. And by that, I mean different. You should never work with someone who thinks like you. They won't add anything new to the thought process. Instead, work with someone who is the polar opposite of you. Opposites do more than just attract; they offer differing views on the same information. This enables you to turn tensions between ideas into useful opportunities.

The more diversity you have in a team, the stronger the ideas will become. Just like in the movie *The Avengers*, where a team of diverse heroes with different superpowers come together to stop catastrophic destruction, I believe in assembling diverse ideation teams to generate world-class ideas. To achieve this, I seek out individuals who bring different perspectives to the process by mixing genders, races and ages. Then I mix up the skill sets, and form partnerships between creatives and data experts, or get sales to work with manufacturing. Or I level the hierarchy and match executives with trainees. You could even team up a priest with an atheist. Or an artist with a mathematician. If you're an American, you could even team up a Democrat with a Republican. This will make your ideation teams so wrong, they're right.

By embracing this approach, your aim should be to create ideation teams that challenge conventional thinking and lead to stronger, more unexpected ideas.

This is the kind of thinking that paired Martha Stewart with Snoop Dogg for the cooking show *Martha & Snoop's Potluck Dinner Party*.

The show premiered in 2016 and lasted for forty episodes and three seasons. The first time I watched it, I realized it was such a clever idea to match a marijuana-smoking rap mogul with a disgraced lifestyle expert. By pairing the right wrong people, the show's producers delivered a reality show that's equal parts ridiculous and surprising at the same time. It definitely brought something special to the staid format of a typical cooking show. Besides the entertaining and awkward banter between the two hosts, it showed that two people from very different backgrounds and cultural experiences could still bond over the time-honoured tradition of sharing a meal. And it was a gentle reminder that differences can be celebrated to create a connection.

When you put diverse people together, you generate more diverse solutions. This helps your thinking to be more robust and multi-faceted than it would be if you were working by yourself or with someone just like you. Organizations that seek excellence know the 'who' is more important than the 'what'. The 'who' are the right wrong people who can adapt to the fast-moving challenges we face in this fast-changing world. It doesn't matter what your corporate vision is, it will fail if you don't first select the right wrong people to help get you there.

And best of all, when opposites get together, you'll be able to observe several things happening.

First, they will complement each other. Filling in the blanks in each other's personal experiences. As a member of the team, you get to learn, feel and experience things you never would have if you'd stayed in your own comfort zone. Second, opposites compensate for each other's weaknesses. When you can't think of a new idea, your partner will often take the idea to a place you would never have thought of. Third, the easiest way to recognize greatness is to work with someone who doesn't think like you do. It opens your eyes to different perspectives and allows you to see a problem in a different light. In the end, you'll generate more ideas, which is what you're trying to do, because when you're brainstorming, quantity is more important than quality. The refining process to get to the quality ideas comes later.

Remember, if you want to find stronger, more unexpected ideas, team up with someone who thinks differently to you.

No One Left Behind

In this short life, we're all in it together. For good or for bad, we need other humans. This is true of ideation as well. We succeed, or we fail, together. So it's important that your ideation team works smoothly, humming and gleaming like a well-oiled machine. And doesn't break down like an old cranky lawnmower.

A 2014 study from Stanford University found that even the mere perception of working collectively on a task could supercharge our performance. Participants in the research who were primed to act collaboratively reported higher engagement levels, lower fatigue levels and a higher success rate.[26]

So here are some easy ways to keep your ideation session in top condition. Before you start a brainstorming session, make sure all participants have been fully briefed on the rules of the space. Everyone needs a clear understanding of what to expect in a brainstorming session. Not everyone is an expert and, many times, there will be participants who are new to the experience. Use a briefing session to ensure everyone is coming along for the ride.

The next thing to do is go through the basics, including a summary of the task ahead, a timeline and a list of deliverables. Ensure everyone knows and follows a simple format to present ideas. Then remind participants to utilize the benefits of the safe ideation space. Reassure them it's a judgement-free zone. Remind them to stay positive and to feel free to have silly ideas. And finally, put the ideation task into context. Explain how it fits into the big picture of what you're trying to achieve. Get people excited about the scope of change their new ideas might generate.

If you've briefed them correctly, they will fail hard, and fail often. Um . . . don't you mean succeed? No, I mean fail. Failure is a critical stepping-stone to great ideation. I guess I should explain the benefits of failure. On the next page.

A Culture of Failure

Failure is my best friend. I love failure. I fail as much as I can, whenever I can. And that's how I find success faster. It sounds counterintuitive, I know, but failure is critical to success. You have to embrace failure, or you will fail. Think of it like trying to solve an outdoor hedge maze. You have to try many paths (and fail), until you find your way to the centre of the maze. We never know which path is correct until we stumble upon the right one.

In the same way, any safe space for brainstorming must include the freedom to fail. The freedom to say something stupid. To suggest something unworkable. We don't reach great ideas in a single step. It's a roundabout journey where we must search many paths that lead to dead ends, until we find the one that doesn't. If you don't fail regularly, you may never reach your destination.

Sir Ken Robinson, who was a British author, wrote: 'If you're not prepared to be wrong, you'll never come up with anything original.'[27] For people to feel brave enough to have an idea, they must work in a criticism-free zone. Our ideas are like our babies. We want to nurture them, and make sure they grow up strong. So when someone crushes our ideas under their boots, it can feel like we've lost something precious. And our natural ability to think of ideas can be stifled. People must be free to share ideas without fear of judgement. They must be free of prejudices about the project, and free of expectations of outcomes.

Encouragement is key. Samuel Beckett, the Irish writer who won the 1969 Nobel Prize in Literature, had this advice: 'Ever tried. Ever failed. No matter. Try again. Fail again. Fail better.'[28] To collide together successfully, we must be free to know that no idea is wrong. They are critical stepping-stones to a great idea. Participants should be open to any possibility, as they won't know at the beginning, what the solution will look like at the end.

If you want to succeed, learn to fail hard and fail often.

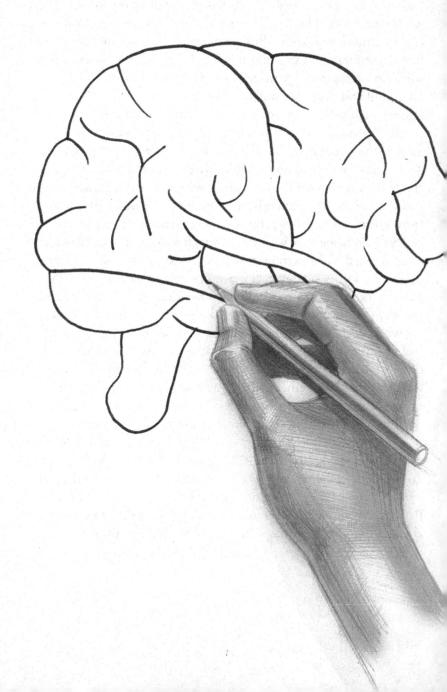

World's Greatest Tools

The best kind of thinking is done face-to-face with another human being. If that's not possible, Zoom can also work as long as the participants bring their brains and a positive attitude. Apart from that, you'll need stacks of paper and pencils. Why? Because doodling is good, and googling is bad. Or to put it another way, writing with pencils (or pens) is a far better way to brainstorm than typing on a keyboard. It's even better than using brainstorming or mind-mapping apps. Let me explain the science behind this idea.

One of the worst habits to arise in the last fifty years is the taking of notes using a laptop or other device. Sure, you can type faster—and don't need to transcribe your handwritten notes later—but your cognitive processing of the information is shallower. Conversely, when you write by hand, you store information slowly, which gives you the time to process the information as you write. This leads to higher quality learning, and is a superior strategy for recalling information later on.

A study by Pam Mueller of Princeton University shows that recall of presentation material is lower when note-takers use laptops instead of pen and paper. Laptop note-takers also perform worse on subsequent testing.[29] Wray Herbert, writing at *Psychological Science*, notes, 'Typing leads to mindless processing. And something about ink and paper prompts students to go beyond merely hearing and recording new information—and instead to process and reframe information in their own words.'[30] Patricia Ann Wade, a learning specialist from Indiana University, who has studied the effects of writing by hand, says that 'Writing entails using the hand and fingers to form letters . . . the sequential finger movements activate multiple regions of the brain associated with processing and remembering information.'[31]

To put all this in simple terms, writing by hand helps you understand concepts and remember them better, because your brain is more deeply involved in the process. Perhaps that's why famous writers—like Neil Gaiman and J.K. Rowling—use pencils to write the first drafts for their stories. Incidentally, pencils were also the preferred writing tools of John Steinbeck, Ernest Hemingway and Vladimir Nabokov.

Personally, I like to use paper to record thoughts because the act of writing and doodling hclps stimulate thinking in ways computer screens never can. Ideas can be mapped organically. You can make connections visually as you look at ideas written on paper and quickly mix-and-match ideas at the speed of thought. Any good ideas can be quickly scribbled down, stuck on a wall and saved for later when you want to review.

Ideas written with pencils are filled with possibility. Nothing is fixed in stone if it's written in pencil. It can be erased and rewritten. You can use pencils to sketch out an idea or doodle a picture. They do not have the permanence of ink and they are one of the most reliable tools to capture fleeting thoughts. Some people even find they help relieve anxiety because you can chew on the end, or tap them like a drumstick.

Pencils have other benefits too. They are cheap and reliable and they can be used for months before you need a new one. You can use them on a deserted island or in the middle of a forest, as they don't require batteries. You can also write with them upside down, while you relax in a bean bag or a hammock.

Of course, there is a time for googling and using computers, but not when you're colliding ideas with another human. Brainstorming with others is not a linear process. Thoughts come to you randomly and are recorded non-sequentially. When done properly, there is very little logic involved. Trying to brainstorm using keyboards (or the internet) is much too logical and limiting. It will only show you what's been done before. Additionally, you'll constantly be distracted by incoming emails and social media updates. You need organic brains and old-fashioned pens for quality, lateral thinking. Then, after a good idea has formed, you can use technology to check the work, improve its execution and share with others.

To summarize, trying to find good ideas using pencils (or pens) is a far superior method than using a keyboard. This is because you can process the information as you write it, remember it better, map ideas organically, make connections visually and easily create pictures and mind-maps, not just words.

As long as you remember to combine paper, pencils and brains, you'll always have access to an infinite number of ideas. *(And don't forget to bring your pencil sharpener and eraser too!)*

Do it in the Dark

When some people have sex, they like to leave the lights on so they see what they're doing. And there are other people who like to have sex with the lights off. I'm not an advocate for either method, as each approach has its pros and cons, but having sex in the dark does deliver an extra benefit to our brain—it allows us the freedom to focus.

Quite simply, the darkness illuminates our imagination. If, for example, we don't like the way we look, darkness allows us to focus on the task at hand without fear of embarrassment. Reducing distractions to our senses, also helps focus our thinking. In fact, if it wasn't for the liberating protection of darkness, many of us might still be virgins.

Great artists and original thinkers are often drawn to the darker hours for the same reasons. The writer Toni Morrison once told *The Paris Review* that watching the night turn to day, with a cup of coffee in hand, made her feel like a 'conduit' of creativity. 'It's not being in the light,' she said, 'it's being there *before it arrives*.'[32]

In 2013, psychologists Anna Steidel and Lioba Werth conducted experiments to measure creativity's response to various lighting schemes. The researchers demonstrated that merely thinking about different types of light influenced a person's creativity. In one experiment, participants spent five minutes describing either a bright or dark location in detail, and then drew a picture of an alien from another galaxy. The aliens drawn by people who'd thought about darkness had more imaginative features—X-rays eyes, for instance, or legs connected to heads—and independent judges rated them as more creative.

Of course, thinking about a dark room is very different from sitting in one. So, in a subsequent experiment, Steidel and Werth arranged a simulated office environment with three different lighting conditions—150 lux (a cloudy day), 500 lux (a typical office) and 1,500 lux (the bright lights used in TV studios). The participants worked on four classic insight problems that require creativity to solve. (The 'candle problem', for instance, asks people to put a candle on a wall using just a box of tacks; the solution requires realizing the box can be tacked to the wall.) People at the dim workspaces solved significantly more problems than those at the bright cubicles.

Steidel and Werth reported some of the first evidence for what ideation masters know by nature: when the lights switch off, something in the brain switches on. 'Apparently, darkness triggers a chain of interrelated processes, including a cognitive processing style, which is beneficial to creativity', the researchers concluded in the September 2013 *Journal of Environmental Psychology*.[33]

In 2012, Ketchum Pleon München—an award-winning global communications consultancy—did an interesting experiment. They wanted to find out what happens when people brainstorm without an important sense—the eye. So they shaded a conference room with cardboard and tape and started brainstorming. The participants and facilitators discovered the introduction of darkness leads to more sensitivity in your remaining senses. According to employee Claudia Geidel, they found that people who think in the dark are more focused on the problem, due to the absence of any visual distraction. The reduction of stimuli freed up the brain's processing power and enabled participants to reach a broader variety of creative solutions.[34]

Sensory deprivation of any kind can make our brains work better. Try visiting a health spa that offers Float Tanks. These are sensory deprivation chambers where you float in a saline water solution, losing the senses of sight, sound and touch. A trance-like state can be experienced that increases imagination, intuition and originality. Bright lights can be good to help us think in rational and scientific ways. But it's low-light situations that help us think in imaginary ways. You don't have to work in total darkness, but neither should you work under a harsh spotlight.

If you normally work under bright fluorescent lights, you could turn them off. If that's not an option, you could wear a blindfold or simply close your eyes. When a friend of mine in Australia wanted to brainstorm and the environment was too bright, he and his team would simply throw sheets over their heads. Although they looked like kids on Halloween dressed like ghosts, they got rid of the bright light, as well as any other visual distractions.

Remember, if you want to increase your creative confidence and find more focus in your thinking, turn off the lights and turn on your mind.

The Importance of NOT Being Earnest

With apologies to Oscar Wilde, I've paraphrased the title to his deliciously satirical play to emphasize the mood your brain needs to be in to brainstorm successfully. It's time we discussed the importance of not being serious. Or the art of being playful.

'But this is an office! We must be professional. This is not the right place for silliness.' I've heard these words said in many non-progressive organizations. They often dismiss play as frivolous, irrelevant and a waste of time. Sadly, they don't realize how wrong they are. Play is critically important for organizations that need to develop new, breakthrough ideas, so they can survive in the ever-connected world of the twenty-first century.

Play is not just important to childhood development, it also plays a vital role in adult life 'building critical skills like systems thinking, creative problem solving, collaboration, empathy and innovation,' according to the National Institute for Play, a Californian non-profit organization dedicated to advancing society's understanding and application of play.[35]

Play unlocks creativity, opens up new perspectives and allows us to 'explore the impossible'. Play creates a safe space where all ideas are welcome, no matter what your job title is or seniority inside an organization. Play enriches creative ideation by creating connections and trust. These connections create a platform where teams can do new and innovative work. Play gets us out of our own heads, and helps turn off the analytical part of our thinking that can lead to 'analysis paralysis'. Play enables us to 'go with the flow'.

Researchers in neuroscience have shown that play is built into the biology of all mammals. Affective neuroscientists, who study how emotions work in the brain, have proven that humans are born with seven primary-process emotional systems, one of which is play. All of these emotional systems are pre-wired in the midbrain, the source of our most basic instincts and motivations. When the play circuits in the midbrain are triggered, the related neurons create a cascade of activity in our higher brain functions. The more often we play, the more those neurons connect and the stronger those pathways get.[36] So every time you are playful when ideating, the better you become at ideating. It's a win-win situation.

Carl Gustav Jung was a very famous Swiss psychiatrist and psychoanalyst who founded analytical psychology. His work has been influential in many fields including psychology, psychiatry, literature, philosophy and religious studies. In one of his essays on psychological types, Jung wrote, 'Out of a playful movement of elements whose interrelations are not immediately apparent, patterns arise which an observant and critical intellect can only evaluate afterwards. The creation of something new is not accomplished by the intellect, but by the play instinct . . .'[37]

He uses a lot of big, fancy words, but what he meant is that the ability to think of new ideas is not based on how logical you are, but based on how playful you can be with your thinking. Quite simply, to come up with new ideas and breakthrough thinking, you need to be in a playful mood. Even when working on serious subjects.

Being too serious while you work can seriously limit your ability to think freely. It causes you to worry too much. *Will the idea be accepted? Is it too expensive? Is it even feasible?* Maybe you worry the idea is different to 'the way things are done around here'. If you suffer from being too earnest, your ideas will never venture far from being 'safe'. You will create ideas that don't rock the boat. And eventually, you'll end up with ideas that are boring, sedate and unsurprising. This kind of earnest thinking is the opposite of what you should be doing.

Instead, you need to be frivolous. If you're not having fun while you collide ideas, you're not doing it right. Keeping the mood light is what makes you ready to play. To play with other people. To play with ideas. And to play with a problem. This playful mindset helps get you into the child-like way of thinking where you don't take things too seriously. This mindset also allows your mind to reach beyond the limits of what's possible. To create ideas that no one has seen before.

If you always approach your ideation sessions with a sense of playful adventure, eventually you'll end up with ideas that are fun, exciting and surprising. Which are the best ideas of all.

Act Childishly

Now that you're not thinking too earnestly, it's time to start acting childishly. Of course, I don't mean being immature, wetting your pants and throwing tantrums. There are enough adults doing that already. I mean reverting back to a child-like state where you explored, spoke your mind, questioned things and didn't make premature judgements.

We often hesitate to suggest ideas because we're worried about being judged. This kills our best ideas. To let your imagination fly, you must stop thinking like an adult and start thinking like a child. Children are risk-takers. Their approach to playing, exploration and their perception of the world lacks our adult fear of failure.

By turning ideation into a playful experience, we can tap into our inner child. Picasso, the famous artist (and nasty misogynist) was thought to have said: 'Every child is an artist. The problem is how to remain an artist after he grows up.'[38]

In America, North Dakota State University researchers Darya Zabelina and Michael Robinson discovered adults tend to be more imaginative when they retain the mindset and behaviours of a child.[39] Before you start ideating, ask everyone to draw a cartoon of the boss. Or play a round of Thumb Wars. Or find out everyone's favourite flavour of ice cream. Find the right level of playfulness that makes you feel ready to play.

And don't forget to doodle. Doodling is a very powerful tool that makes us use multiple learning modalities all at once. It involves hand-eye coordination, visual and touch stimulation, as well as drawing, writing and reading skills. Doodling is a powerful tool for tapping into subconscious connections not apparent on the surface. It engages your subconscious ideation skills and often leads to unexpected solutions.

If you want to improve your ideation, regress back to the state of mind you had as a child—when nothing was impossible.

Because when you act and think like a child, you'll ideate at the highest level.

KEEP CALM AND DON'T BREAK RULES

Unbreakable Rules

Rule One: Dig Lots of Holes

Have you ever wanted to feel like a miner working underground? Well, now's your chance. Coming up with ideas is a lot like digging for gold. You dig in a lot of places with no gold, until one day, your shovel hits a big, juicy nugget. Sometimes, it feels like you will never find the gold, but the secret is persistence. If you dig long enough in enough places, sooner or later you will hit the jackpot. You just have to keep digging.

Walter S. Mallory—a colleague of Thomas Edison—tells an insightful story about persistence. Edison and his team of researchers had been trying to develop a nickel-iron battery for over five months. Mallory arrived for a visit, and learnt they had tried over nine thousand experiments, and were no closer to solving the problem. Feeling sympathetic, Mallory said: 'Isn't it a shame that with the tremendous amount of work you have done you haven't been able to get any results?' Quick as a flash, and with a smile on his face, Edison replied: 'Results! Why, man, I have gotten a lot of results! I know several thousand things that won't work'. [40]

What Edison knew is that ideation involves exploring as many ideas as possible. The more ideas you have, the better your final idea will be. If you have a hundred ideas, ninety-five will be terrible, four will be okay, and one might be brilliant. We keep digging until we find gold. Keep digging until your shovel breaks.

Rule Two: There Are No Silly Ideas

All ideas, both good and bad, are the stepping-stones on the path
to great ideas. It is not, as some people think, a series of 'perfect'
ideas that lead to the most perfect. There are many deviations on
the path. We must take many wrong turns to find the right path.
But people won't feel comfortable to suggest a 'wrong' idea if
they think they will be subjected to harsh judgement. Who would?
We all have feelings.

To brainstorm productively and get to the good stuff, we
must feel free to express ideas and also be silent enough to listen
to them. Like the title of my favourite George Michael album,
we must 'Listen Without Prejudice'. Instead of feeling like we are
being judged on ideas, we must feel free to bounce them around
like tennis balls. With each bounce adding new possibilities to the
idea. Then, sooner or later, the idea will bounce a certain way and
suddenly a great problem-solving idea will become evident to you.

To keep the flow of ideas going, offer an abundance of
positivity. Never criticize ideas, or the wonderfully fragile humans
who share them. Be gentle with your ideation partners. Cynicism
can stifle free thought, while negativity turns off the tap, seals the
chamber and throws away the key.

If you hear an idea you don't like, suggest another idea.
And keep the flow of silly ideas going until you reach the idea
that's not silly.

Rule Three: Throw Logic Out The Window

Logic is a wonderful thing. Logic helps us in so many ways. We couldn't survive without it. Many people love logic, but I always have an irresistible urge to strangle it, set it on fire and toss it off a cliff. *Gee, that's a bit harsh, Guan.* Perhaps. But there is a very logical reason why I dislike logic. After fear, logic is the greatest threat to creative conflict. Logic kills the kind of thinking that takes you somewhere unexpected. Logic kills ideas before they're fully formed. Logic is a murderer!

As humans, we're always in such a rush to find solutions. We tend to stop halfway through an ideation session to see if any of our ideas have solved the problem. This can be problematic when trying to come up with ideas. This 'stop-and-start' approach means you never get your brain operating at full capacity. Thinking logically is a great way to kill ideas. To kill the kind of thinking that leads to great ideas.

My advice is to never stop in the middle of a brainstorming session to analyse the quality of an idea. That's like throwing a spanner into a jet engine. Not recommended if you're trying to fly. Any critical analysis breaks the magic of lateral, free-moving thoughts. When you stop thinking creatively and start thinking logically, you switch off the power to think outside the box. For the best results, evaluation of ideas should happen afterwards, once a session is over. Save logic for later.

Much, much later.

Get in the Mood

The last stage is to prepare our mind for ideation. We need to be open and receptive to unusual thoughts. Washing our brains with a little meditation might be a great technique to clear our minds. But then what?

The first thing to do is abolish job titles, so there are no pre-existing roles for people to play. The boss is not the boss. The trainees are not trainees. In ideation sessions, everyone is on the same level. The reason we do this is to allow ideas to flow freely. For example, a trainee working with a boss might only suggest safe ideas, or ideas they think will impress. Likewise, a boss may steer clear of suggesting strange ideas, for fear of appearing stupid or not in control. Both of these situations destroy the free flow of ideas, and lead to suboptimal solutions. The ideation space must be a neutral one.

We also have to manage stage fright. Bouncing ideas around with others can feel frightening. Do not underestimate this fear; for some people, it is a debilitating phobia. According to Sarah Gershman in *Harvard Business Review*, she said even the most confident public speakers have to 'disarm their panic buttons' when facing an audience.[41]

The secret is to stop thinking about our fears and start thinking about helping the audience. The article provides three techniques on how to do this, which are extremely helpful. It advises us to think about the audience's needs, refocus our brain to want to help the audience and, lastly, to make eye contact. It's worth reading this article and sharing some of its fear-busting strategies before commencing the brainstorming session.

Additionally, to help break or overcome any remaining awkwardness, start every session with a joke. Tell a funny story. This acts as an icebreaker and gives people the confidence to have lots of ideas, no matter how silly they might sound.

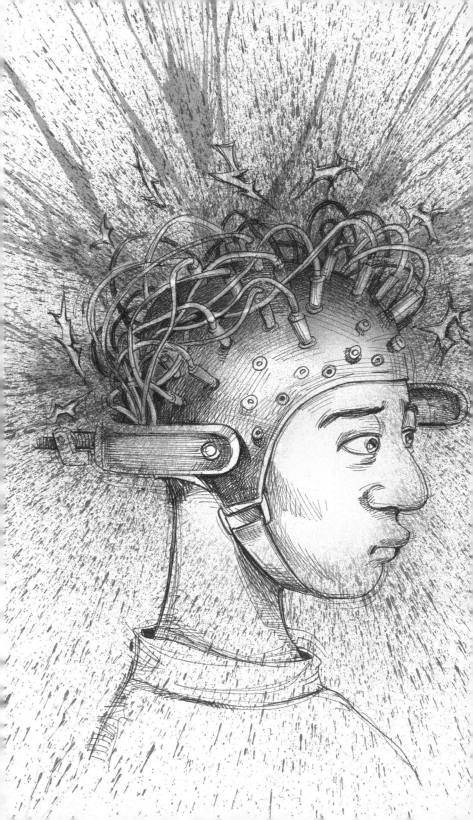

Your Ride Has Now Been Pimped

You're starting to look like a mighty fine ideation machine. Your ideation pistons are firing cleanly and you've got a fresh set of tires ready to hit the road. There are still a few kinks to work out and a few rough bits to polish, but you're finally starting to look like you're ready for some head-on collisions.

First, you changed the way you think to become open to all the wonders of the world. Now, you know how to create a safe space to brainstorm. You've given the right people the world's greatest tools to enable them to act childishly and get in the mood. Armed with unbreakable rules and a culture of failure, you're finally ready to brainstorm. This is where the rubber hits the road. Now that the preparation work has been completed, you are ready to learn some of the non-mystical techniques of ideation.

In the next chapter, you will discover all of the techniques I use to come up with ideas. These techniques are the highly flammable jet fuel I like to splash around to help get the creative fires burning. As you read the following pages, you may want to be extra careful and wear something non-flammable. It goes without saying that these brainstorming techniques are highly dangerous. They act like unstable dynamite, so you may want to turn the next page slowly and carefully. And as all the following techniques involve head-on collisions, you may want to put on your crash helmet too.

For good ideas and true innovation, you need human interaction, conflict, argument, debate.

Margaret Heffernan [42]

Interview with INTERNATIONAL MAESTRO Matt Eastwood

Before we get into my brainstorming techniques, let's hear from an international giant in the advertising industry—Matt Eastwood. He rose from humble beginnings as a copywriter in Sydney, to lead the creative output of several agencies, including becoming the chief creative officer of DDB New York and worldwide chief creative officer of J. Walter Thompson. His most recent position was global chief creative officer of McCann Health. At Cannes Lions 2020/21, the agency won 17 Lions, a Grand Prix and was named Agency of the Year.

Guan: *Hi Matt, you've worked in the advertising industry for thirty-five years. How important is creative conflict to the creative process?*
Matt: Creative conflict is really about diversity of thinking. It's important to bring diverse and differing points of view to the ideation process. Without conflict, or diverse thinking, we can never truly push our work into new and uncharted territory. This is essential, if we hope to stand out in the crowded space of contemporary marketing. The beauty of this is that it very much reflects the current thinking around diversity and inclusion. Diversity challenges us and creates the necessary positive conflict we need, to bring to life bold, new ideas.

Guan: *Learning to mash up ideas is hard. What can I do to train my brain to think that way?*
Matt: There are some really easy tools and processes that you can use to encourage your brain to learn how to mash up ideas. One of my favourites is simply bringing two very different people together to see what they can create. Another of my favourite techniques is using an app like Brian Eno's Oblique Strategies. It poses simple challenges like 'turn it upside down' or 'remove

a restriction' in order to force you to think differently about a problem or creative idea you're developing.

Guan: *What's your favourite brainstorming technique to collide ideas?*
Matt: One of my favourite techniques for creating new ideas is a technique I learned from Tony Award-winning musical writer, Jeff Marx. When I worked at Y&R New York, I was curious about the process of creating a musical, so I asked Jeff to come and talk to the creative department about his method. Along with many pearls of wisdom, he talked about the notion of taking another idea and 'kicking sand over it'. He demonstrated the technique by explaining how he created the main song from *Avenue Q*, his hugely awarded Broadway musical. He said he wanted a song like 'Rainbow Connection', which explained the overall premise of the show. But what he actually did to create the song was surprising and brilliant. Basically, he took the music from 'Rainbow Connection' and wrote new lyrics to it. Once he'd constructed the song, he said he 'kicked sand over it' to make it different. He changed the music here and there until eventually he had the song, 'What do you do with a BA in English?'. And trust me, the new song is unrecognizable as 'Rainbow Connection'. He even sung the lyrics to the new song, with the music from 'Rainbow Connection' and it matched perfectly. I loved this idea of taking something you know as inspiration and changing it to make something completely new.

Guan: *What are the dangers of collaboration? And how can we create a culture of collaboration within a company?*
Matt: 'Groupthink' can be an idea killer. Or, at the very least, it can generate bland ideas. Which is why it is so important to introduce conflict to collaboration. To make it work, we need to take inspiration from 'improv'. The philosophy of improv is 'yes . . . and', which is exactly how we need to behave when

we collaborate. Don't shut ideas down because they don't reflect your point of view. Build on ideas. Say 'yes . . . and' as often as you can. This is particularly important when you are working with people from different cultural, social, or economic backgrounds. By definition, our ideas and our reference points will be different because our backgrounds are different. We need to embrace this and say 'yes . . . and'.

Guan: *Yes . . . and thank you, Matt.*

Matt has highlighted some important points. First, he has explained why diversity of thinking is crucial to creative conflict. And second, he has shared two great brainstorming techniques, in the form of 'kicking sand on it', and using the improvising technique of 'yes . . . and' to build ideas and explore further. Now it's my turn to get naked. In the next chapter, I will finally expose my trade secrets and reveal the dangerous techniques I use to brainstorm ideas.

Chapter Seven

UNSTABLE DYNAMITE DON'T SHAKE BOOK

(Where I divulge dangerous ways
to come up with ideas).

Head-On Collisions For Crash-Test Dummies

By now, you have a good understanding of what creative conflict is. You've trained your brain and prepared the right environment. But when you try to begin crashing ideas together . . . nothing happens. You're staring at a blank piece of paper. And your mind is blank. How exactly do we create ideas?

There's nothing quite as terrifying as staring at an empty page and thinking you have to fill it with good ideas. Just the thought is enough to make some people freeze in terror. Luckily, none of them are reading this book. It's just you and me. And we have hearts full of courage because we know the path is dangerous, but survivable.

The most common way to find inspiration is from crashing ideas together. With enough practice, it can be done all alone. But working with another person can really make the process deliver spectacular results. Instead of having one set of knowledge to work with, having a partner automatically doubles that knowledge base. And more than that, when you add the two sets of knowledge together, it creates a third set that is a hybrid of both. This creative conflict—with two brains chipping away at the problem—takes your brain on a lateral journey it couldn't make on its own. This makes the process faster and leads to more original thinking. It's the secret to finding the very best ideas. Ideas that are not 'mine' or 'yours', but a melding of two or more minds, creating an idea more powerful than a regular human can create by themselves.

And once you know how to do that, you'll find that coming up with ideas is easy. And with a little practice, it's fast too. Beginning on the next page, in all their naked glory, are my own explosive techniques you can use to smash ideas together. Handle them with care.

Start With the Worst Ideas

The biggest barrier to ideation is not your brain. You have an awesome brain. The biggest barrier is fear. People are scared to share ideas, because they don't want to look stupid. Scared that everyone will laugh at them. But if you're scared of looking stupid, you'll never have the courage to think of the unexpected. Even though you may have created a safe environment, you may still need other techniques to help remove the fear barrier.

We all want to find the best idea, the one that everyone loves. But that's a hard thing to do in one step. Instead, start your ideation session by trying to think of the worst idea. Think of expensive ideas. And impossible ideas. The ones that are grandiose or could never be implemented. Think of the silliest ideas. The one that will never work. The one that would be fun to try. The one your boss will hate.

Pressure can add unwanted fear too. One time, when preparing a huge, multi-million-dollar presentation, my team was stuck and couldn't think of any good ideas. We were too frightened of failure. Suddenly, I stood up and told everyone to forget about the budget and whether the client would like it. Then I suggested the craziest, dumbest idea, which made everyone laugh and lightened the mood. I encouraged everyone to let go of their doubts and write down their wildest ideas on the board. One after another, shy voices became sure of themselves. This resulted in a flood of new ideas, leading to a long list of plans we were excited and proud to present.

The main purpose of this technique is to break the fear of ideation. To destroy the barriers of fear and criticism. I find ideation sessions are more productive when I start with the worst ideas.

Anyone can generate great ideas. When they start without fear.

Drain Your Brain

We often waste time thinking in expected ways. Solving problems using old solutions or techniques. We need to get rid of these obvious solutions before we can reach the good ideas. With normal thinking, this takes up a lot of valuable time. So how do we get to the good stuff faster? Simply drain your brain. It's a quick technique, and how I start most ideation sessions.

Grab a pencil and some paper and find a quiet spot. Spend twenty minutes coming up with a hundred ideas. That's only twelve seconds per idea. Not a lot of time, and that's the point. This technique forces you to work at lightning speed. Barely thinking. Just blurting out silly ideas. Unworkable ideas. Unintelligible ideas. When you're finished, you'll notice something unsettling. Practically all of the ideas will be terrible. I mean, just woeful. But that's okay. Because that is what this technique is designed to do.

It helps you scrape out the gunk in your brain and forces you to get past the garbage-thinking. It removes ideas that are tired, expected and unoriginal. At the end of this process, you would have gone past the expected outcomes and be ready to think of something completely new. Once you've exhausted your well of obvious ideas, the less obvious and more insightful ideas will surface. Not bad for a twenty-minute exercise.

By the way, I stole this technique from David Droga. In 1996, he became the regional creative director of Saatchi Asia. On our first project together, he demanded each creative team draw and fill up hundred square boxes with ideas, keeping none empty. We were only given one hour to complete the task, so I was stressed trying to fill all the boxes. After eighty boxes, I could see the transformation of my ideas starting to get better and better. Out of a hundred ideas, at least five were excellent.

Droga's effort to drain our brains paid off on the world stage when Saatchi & Saatchi Singapore beat all other agencies outside the USA to win the coveted Advertising Age International Agency of the Year.

What If . . .

When you are first trying to think of ideas, the beginning of any ideation session can feel devoid of inspiration. Of course, once you get going, it's fairly easy to keep generating ideas. But how do we start the session? How do we get over the initial hump of having no ideas at all, when participants are feeling cold and uninspired? For me, I like to start every ideation session with my two favourite words in the English language. What if . . .?

What if we did it this way? What if we did it that way? What if we found an idea no one's ever seen before? Of all the techniques to crash ideas together, 'what if . . .?' is my personal favourite. I use these words on a daily basis to explore ideas. What if cows give milk in different flavours? What if elephants could fly? What if I can't think of any ideas and I lose my job? Yikes!

Margaret Atwood, the author of *The Handmaid's Tale*, believes future narratives hinge on 'what if . . .?' premises, an element central to speculative writing. This concept is traceable from the 'what if . . .?' tragedies of Euripides to Shakespeare's fairyland comedies, and it persisted into the twentieth century. Writers such as Philip K. Dick and Malorie Blackman have used it to reinterpret historical events. This technique, known as counterfactual thinking,[43] is a literary device and a psychological tool. It encourages us to envision alternative futures, fostering creative planning and the development of new habits.

'What if? . . .' helps you to think of the consequences of actions. It allows you to visualize the future. And it opens your mind to new realities and fantastical possibilities.

Use this phrase often at the start of an ideation session and, in no time at all, you'll find the ideas will start to flow thick and fast.

Take a Dump

Sometimes it's hard to think of ideas using words. There are lots of us out there who think visually. So sometimes it's easier to find ideas using visuals instead. That's because our brains process visuals 60,000 times faster than text.[44] If words are slowing your ideation down, take a visual dump.

One of the reasons I wanted to be an art director was that I love to tell visual stories. So when I begin to think, I think of visuals first. I always create a visual mood board that describes the idea and reflects how the finished project might look or feel. This stimulates my imagination. You can easily create a mood board by searching images on Google, using AI like Midjourney, or looking at a stock photo library.

For example, if I am coming up with ideas to sell hot and spicy fries, I look for visuals that best represent hot and spicy. Often, selecting the right pictures for a mood board can show what your finished idea 'feels' like. A picture can often communicate in a way that words can't.

Is the problem you're trying to solve expensive or prestigious? Or does it feel cheap, like a second-hand store? Is it active or passive? Is it night or day? Is it like a comforting old friend, or an exciting lover? Find visuals that feel right to you. The ones that speak to you in a way you can't define. Trying to define your problem visually can often lead you to a visual that sparks ideas.

Here's another secret. Your ideation plan doesn't have all the answers. Sometimes your bosses don't either. Take the time to search the web for anything that relates to your product or service. A single visual may be all the stimulation you need.

Visuals have a way of sparking ideas that can't be achieved with words. Taking a visual dump and creating a mood board often leads to unintended, yet powerful solutions.

Hijacking

The easiest way to come up with an idea is to hijack something from pop culture. This involves taking a current trend, or something familiar, and twisting it for your ideation purposes. I mean, why bother stressing about solutions on your own, when you can hijack someone else's thinking processes? This is one of the fastest ways to get an idea.

The way to do it is to find themes and trends that share traits with your business problem. Popular things, like a fashion or TikTok trend. Well-known things, like a song or movie character. Even nursery rhymes can be hijacked if they're famous enough.

A great example is the Melbourne singer, Gotye—real name Wouter (Wally) De Backer—born in Belgium, but who now calls Australia home.[45] Gotye 'hijacked' the melody from the nursery rhyme 'Baa Baa, Black Sheep' for his song, 'Somebody That I Used to Know'.[46]

Of course, you need to make the idea your own, i.e., change it enough so that the original creator does not consider taking any legal steps citing copyright infringement. Then you're good to go.

But remember—when you tap into pop culture, what's popular today won't be popular tomorrow. Social media trends are constantly evolving, making timing crucial for trend hijacking.

During the 2013 Super Bowl, when a power outage occurred, Oreo's marketing team tweeted a picture of a solitary Oreo in the dark with the caption, 'Power out? No problem. You can still dunk in the dark.'[47] This message hijacked the power outage and reminded people of Oreo's classic 'dunk in milk' ritual. Despite not being a paid commercial, the tweet became one of the most-talked-about advertisements associated with the Super Bowl that year.

So keep up with the news and understand the trends. Stay current with your customers, and find out what gets them talking. Then, hijack it.

HAPPY ACCIDENT. THE PROCESS.

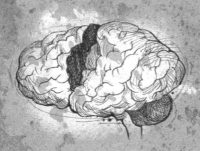

OPEN MIND

UNEXPECTED EVENT

SEE THE POTENTIAL

TAKE THE INITIATIVE

AMPLIFY THE IDEA

EVALUATE THE IDEA

The Happy Accident

Ideation often happens by accident. This is sometimes known as serendipity. As we travel through the world, thought-provoking events often present themselves. But we only see them when we have an open mind. When we stay curious and observant. Observing the world around us, exploring why things fail, just as eagerly as why they work.

How it happens is simple. First, you begin with a curious mind. Then one day, you observe an unexpected event. Within the event, you see a potential idea. So you explore and define the idea. And then you evaluate the idea. And while the process is simple, it may take years or decades of work.

In 1666, a young man was sitting in his garden. His name was Isaac Newton. What he didn't know was he was about to make a random observation that would lead to the discovery of gravity. Newton witnessed an apple fall from a tree. He wondered why the apple always fell perpendicularly to the ground. This train of thought set off a chain of events that ultimately led him to publish a comprehensive theory of gravity.

In an English laboratory in 1928, a happy accident changed the course of medicine. Alexander Fleming, a bacteriologist from St Mary's Hospital London, was talking to a colleague when he noticed an area around a fungus on an agar plate in which the bacteria did not grow. He decided to find out why and, in the process, discovered penicillin. This happy accident resulted from Fleming's observant eye and curious mind.

Once you begin to observe the world around you with an open mind and a ravenous curiosity, then you will find yourself exploring random observations, happy accidents and failed experiments. And great ideas will follow.

That's So Random

How can we think of a new thought when our minds work in predictable ways? For example, if we are trying to think of an idea that goes with 'dog', our mind may think of barking, fur, dog collar, dog bowl, dog house, etc. These are the logical associations our mind goes to first. But when we follow well-worn paths, we tend to end up with similar outcomes. What if we could force ourselves to create new connections in our brains? What new ideas would that create?

According to the Oxford Dictionary, there are 171,146 words in the English language.[48] Each word has its own unique meaning. But most of us only have a vocabulary of around 42,000 words (roughly 25 per cent of the language).[49] This means there are a lot of good words out there that we never think about. Let's use them. First, buy an old-fashioned printed dictionary. Then, open it at a random page and put your finger on a random word. The word you find must be used to come up with an idea for whatever you're working on. It's not as easy as it sounds. And, sometimes, you'll find it impossible. But if you get stuck, choose another random word. If you like, continue choosing random words until one sparks an idea.

By using this technique of random word-association, you force yourself to think in ways that you wouldn't normally. This opens up new pathways of thinking, helping to make unpredictable connections and increasing your brainpower. It allows your lateral thinking mind to find a new idea and, afterwards, your logical mind can work out the steps needed to make it happen.

This banana, taped to a wall, sold for €120,00

That's So Random, Too

If you don't have an old-fashioned dictionary, there's another random technique you can use. But for this, you'll need a willing participant. That's right, you can also unlock random ideation techniques using the brains of others. All you need to do is play a word game. Think of the games you might play with children on a long car trip. Like Word Chain, where the first person names a country, then the next person has to say a country that starts with the last letter of the previous word, such as 'France . . . Ethiopia . . . Australia'.

When you try this game in the office with colleagues, start by using random nouns. You might end up with a list of words like, 'chair . . . robot . . . tree . . . elephant'. Then, like the dictionary trick, you force yourself to use these random words to connect with the problem you are trying to solve. What attributes of the random word could be applied to your problem? Using the words from the list above, 'chair' could lead to stability, 'robot' could lead to automation, 'tree' could lead to connectivity and 'elephant' could lead to memory cards.

It sounds crazy the first time you try it. But once you've done it a few times, you'll see the value in using random techniques to force your brain to be unpredictable. Even if you don't stumble on a great idea at first, you will gain an instant benefit. You will teach yourself how to approach problems from unexpected angles.

Steal Ideas

Are you alone? Is anyone in the room with you? Take a moment to make sure the police aren't watching, because we're about to steal ideas. To clarify, I don't mean getting inspired by someone else's ideas, or copying their ideas. I mean stealing them outright.

The only rule? Don't steal from your own industry. Steal from everyone else. Steal from business, sport and culture. Steal from history, politics and nature. Find great ideas that solve similar problems to yours and re-skin them to your situation.

The world is awash with great ideas and clever solutions to age-old problems. If you dig around a bit, you'll discover that the problem you're trying to solve has already been solved many times throughout history. Find out how they did it. How can you apply their solution to your problem? Studying someone else's great idea will often help you discover the missing piece from your own puzzle.

If you're trying to find cost efficiencies, investigate how other businesses manage costs. If you are trying to improve sales, learn how other industries improve sales. What is it about their solutions that can be applied to your problem? Don't waste time solving a problem if someone's already solved it for you. Find the revolutionary or breakthrough nature of someone else's thinking. Then steal it and apply the same thinking to your project. Remember, a simple idea from one industry can enhance the customer experience when used in another.

For example, in the US, automated teller machines (ATMs) are usually associated with banks. Before the mass-adoption of cashless transactions, ATMs were added to banks to give their customers the added services of 24-hour access to cash, and other banking tools. Sprinkles Bakery thought the idea of '24-hour access' was great. So they stole this idea and applied it to their own business model. They created their own 24-hour cupcake ATM.

Because they rightly surmised that in this tough life, we sometimes need a cupcake at 3 a.m. And even if we don't, it's comforting to know that one is available. By stealing the ATM concept, Sprinkles enhanced their customer's experience and demonstrated a progressive, caring attitude.[50]

When Safelite, a US auto glass repair company, was looking for ways to improve their customer experience, they copied Uber. Specifically, they copied one of the features that Uber offers, which is tracking how far away is your ride. Safelite knew their customers' time was precious, and they realized that no one likes having to wait around, not knowing when a technician is going to arrive and repair your car. So they added a tracking mechanism to their app. Now, when Safelite technicians are en route to repair a vehicle, their customers can track where they are. This was a very convenient and thoughtful way to improve their customer's experience.[51] And stealing ideas is always fun.

Of course, not all theft happens in North America. In the capital of Argentina, Buenos Aires, the Uptown Nightclub wanted to differentiate their bar and restaurant experience. They wanted a unique environment that had never been seen before and they wanted to give the club a more international flavour. So they thought about a few different options before finally settling on the subway stations of North America. Specifically, they chose to copy the look and feel of New York's subway stations, due to the fact that they have appeared in countless films.

The Uptown Nightclub stole the whole look and experience of New York's subway stations and designed a club that looks like a subway station, complete with a subway car that patrons pass through before entering the club. This dramatic makeover led to an increased number of customers who wanted to visit the club, just to enjoy the 'subway' experience and take a few selfies next to the uniquely distinctive decor.[52]

Stealing—or repurposing—ideas that are already successful in other industries, is a great way to find ideas that are already proven to work, and one that will add value to your own company's customer experience. It's what I like to call a no-brainer. Not only is stealing ideas from other industries a great technique for generating ideas, it's also a timesaving life hack since you have a proven idea that's ready to be implemented.

So, like every other technique I've described, feel free to steal it.

Have Fun With the Living Dead

One of the most fun techniques I use to generate ideas is to think in oxymorons. What is an oxymoron? It's when you join contrasting words to create a new word or phrase. Oxymorons often reveal deeper meanings. Exposing the double-sided existence of things. Writers have used them throughout history to describe inherent conflicts and incongruities. Some examples of oxymorons are 'only choice', 'devout atheist', 'awfully good' and 'bittersweet'.

Oxymorons, like the 'living dead', can seem absurd, yet they also make perfect sense at the same time. This duality helps us to think differently. Framing an idea as an oxymoron is a playful technique to get your brain working in unusual ways. It creates a whimsy to your thinking, and helps you get in touch with your inner child. For example, if you decide to frame a problem as 'seriously funny' or 'pretty ugly', it can radically change how you approach the solution.

We can learn the power of the oxymoron from no less an expert than William Shakespeare. In his tragic love story, *Romeo & Juliet*, the star-crossed lovers are from two warring families. Imagine how conflicted these two must have been? Falling in love with your enemy? To convey these strong, yet conflicted, feelings Shakespeare used a generous dose of oxymorons. Romeo describes his feelings as 'heavy lightness', 'sick health' and 'cold fire'. Juliet describes parting from her lover as a 'sweet sorrow'.

These juxtapositions poetically describe the couple's deep, yet conflicted feelings.

In 1964, when Paul Simon wrote a song about cultural alienation and the inability of people to communicate, he called it 'The Sound of Silence'. It became the first big hit for the American folk rock band Simon & Garfunkel. In 1968, when George A. Romero titled his movie about monsters that were both alive and dead, he called it *Night of the Living Dead*. And a whole new genre of film was born.

Oxymorons are particularly useful for naming things. There are many books, songs and movies that use oxymorons to capture the conflicted essence of their stories. You can see a few examples on the following page. But what if you don't work in these creative industries, how can you use oxymorons in your business?

You could begin by trying to think of a few oxymorons to describe your business problem. Think about what your company is known for, and then add the opposite word to create a new phrase. Like 'deafening silence' for vacuum cleaners. Or 'almost exactly' for a budget airline. Or 'properly ridiculous' for a comedy club.

At JWT India, my team needed to create a film for a new soap with a captivating fragrance. But we had a problem. Fragrance is invisible. How do you visualize the invisible? Who could capture beauty beyond what the eye can see? An oxymoron held the answer. Use a blind photographer. And just like that, we had the idea for the film.[53]

Thinking in oxymorons opens new paths to explore. Oxymorons help us play with language and meaning. And they make us look at problems from a unique perspective. This refreshes our brain and gives us a new source of ideas and directions to play with.

The word 'oxymoron' is itself an oxymoron, derived from the Greek words 'oxys' (meaning sharp) and 'moros' (meaning dull).

MOVIE TITLES

Urban Cowboy (1980)
Wrong is Right (1982)
True Lies (1994)
Intimate Strangers (2004)
30 Days of Night (2007)
Definitely, Maybe (2008)
Everlasting Moments (2008)
Beautiful Disaster (2023)

BOOK TITLES

Big Little Lies by Liane Moriarty
Small Great Things by Jodi Picoult
Midnight Sun by Stephenie Meyer
Genuine Fraud by E. Lockhart
Cruel Kindness by Walter Trobisch
Jumbo Shrimp by Bruce Johnson
Awfully Appetizing by Rick Reinert
Original Copy by Alastair Gordon

SONG TITLES

'Forever Young' by Rod Stewart
'Civil War' by Guns 'n' Roses
'Set Fire to the Rain' by Adele
'Foolish Wisdom' by Tom Odell
'Bitter Sweet Symphony' by The Verve
'Burning Ice' by Yngwie Malmsteen
'Open Secret' by Selena Gomez
'Silent Scream' by Anna Blue

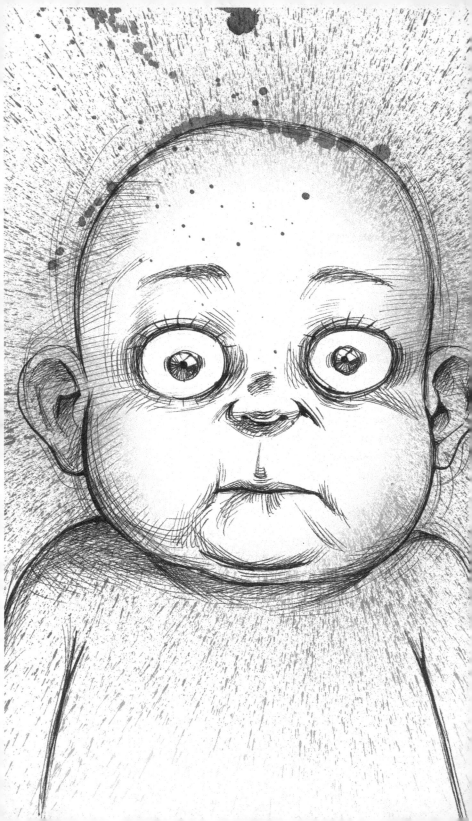

Throw Stink Bombs

Sometimes people get stuck trying to think of something new. Maybe they've run out of ideas. Or maybe they're a little sleepy after lunch. For whatever reason, the free flow of ideas dissipates, the energy in the room starts to plummet and the ideation grinds to a halt. How can we get the flow back?

This is the perfect time to throw a few stink bombs into the room. These are ideas, words or actions that provoke powerful reactions. These reactions increase the energy levels of participants and get everyone's brains refocused on the problem at hand.

Your brain is like a super-computer that loves spotting patterns and reacting based on past experiences. Our brains get stuck in old ways of thinking. This is the time to become provocative, suggesting a course of action that would lead to certain doom. You might tell a joke or advocate for an outcome that is the opposite of what you are trying to achieve. You might even challenge a belief in the room that causes people to get agitated.

Once, when working on an insurance ad, we were having trouble getting started. So I started saying things like, 'What if your husband died from cancer?' and 'What if your child became a paraplegic?' Suddenly it became personal. People were triggered and became emotional. We threw away our predictable ideas and started thinking of unpredictable ideas filled with real emotions.

Crazy, right? But these 'stink bombs' are a wake-up call for your brain. It's like splashing cold water on your face. When you throw stink bombs into an ideation session, people become more alert. These provocations make people forget their old way of thinking. They will pay keen attention to your outrageous words. In their minds, they'll be thinking, 'Wow, that person really shouldn't be saying this kind of stuff'. Which is exactly the kind of mental circuit breaker you need.

This uncomfortable, awkward feeling will energize the ideation session, and help people break out of old ways of thinking, so they can create something new.

Opposite Day

Are you still stuck in a rut? Need another technique to find new ideas? Try taking whatever you're working on and start thinking what the opposite would be.

Any conflicting 'fish-out-of-water' experience is a rich source for ideation. Trying to improve your supply-chain issues? What if you moved your business further away from your suppliers? Designing a new steel pylon? What if it's made from glass instead? If I'm a firefighter in a desert, how could I fight the fire without water? Let's say you're working on a fashion idea. How would that work in a nudist colony? Maybe you're trying to show off a new product. How would you do it without using photos? Perhaps you're trying to improve banking practices. How would the bank operate in a world with no money?

When you take an idea and put it somewhere it doesn't belong, it can reveal hidden strengths and weaknesses. Australian author Aaron Blabey wrote a bestselling kid's book series called *The Bad Guys* about a group of 'bad guy' animals (shark, wolf, snake and piranha) on a quest to show they were really the 'good guys'. When DreamWorks turned the series into a movie in 2022, the author gave an interview to promote the film and explained his creative process: 'There are no new ideas, but there's always new context. And if you can take two things that have never quite been put together quite like that before, you can come up with something really interesting.'[54]

Thinking of hypothetical opposing conflict situations forces you to think of solutions to non-existent problems. It takes you away from standard modes of thinking and leads you to fresh ideas that stimulate new ways of solving problems.

Another way to think of 'opposite' solutions is to try 'reverse brainstorming'. The way this works is that you begin by trying to identify ways you could cause, or worsen your business problem.

Instead of asking yourself 'How do I solve this problem?' ask, 'How could I ensure our customers hate our product?'. You then reverse these ideas to find solutions you hadn't thought of before. This technique is particularly useful when your ideation team has trouble coming up with ideas quickly, when you want people to let go of their preconceived notions and when you want people to step out of their comfort zone and find new ways to solve a problem.

We can see instances of reverse brainstorming in the way modern factories are designed. In the past, workers would move around machines and components when they were building things. This was laborious and productivity was low. An idea was formed to reverse the workflow. Workers would stay in a fixed workplace while components were moved in front of them. Using reverse brainstorming, the idea of assembly lines was developed and efficiency was improved.

Most people think Henry Ford invented the modern assembly line, but in fact, the first person to utilize this concept was Ransom E. Olds. In 1901, he designed a stationary assembly line to create the first mass-produced automobile, the Oldsmobile Curved Dash. This new approach to building automobiles enabled Olds to increase his factory's output by over 500 per cent.[55] Today, most modern manufacturing involves the use of assembly lines. It has helped to reduce manufacturing costs and dramatically reduced the rate of injuries.

On the negative side, the assembly line also increased social alienation and boredom amongst workers. And it created new problems like repetitive strain injury. So while it was a great idea for capitalism, it wasn't so great for the worker. Automation, robots and AI may help to solve some of these problems.

Reverse thinking not only revolutionized manufacturing, it also led to a revolution in medicine. Edward Jenner, a nineteenth-century English physician, spent years looking for a cure for smallpox. But after exploring all the avenues available to him, he reached a point where he couldn't make progress. So he decided to try a little reverse brainstorming. In a remarkable shift of thinking, Jenner decided to focus on people who had <u>never</u> contracted smallpox, instead of those who had.

During his investigations, Jenner learned that dairymaids (women who milked cows) rarely fell ill with smallpox. What was the source of their immunity? Further examination revealed most dairymaids had previously contracted cowpox, a similar yet less severe disease. Jenner realized that cowpox acted as a form of 'vaccination', providing protection against the more dangerous smallpox. This realization led Jenner to develop the concept of 'vaccinating' individuals, laying the foundation for the modern practice of vaccination.[56]

By embracing the opposite perspective and shifting his attention to those unaffected by smallpox, Jenner made a ground-breaking discovery that revolutionized the field of medicine.

And that my friends, is every technique I use to brainstorm. I feel so exposed right now having revealed my secrets. But if that's still not enough for you, turn the page for seven more tips.

Personal tics that make me tick

Still need more brainstorming tricks to make ideas? *Gosh, you're relentless!* Okay, your wish is my command. Here are seven simple things I like to do to keep the ideas flowing.

Walk the Room

I can't sit still. So when I think, I need to walk to stimulate my mind. I also like to stick ideas on the wall. Then other participants can walk around the room and look at the ideas on the wall. This is a great way to add energy to a very sleepy room.

Talk Rubbish

Don't you hate it when the flow of ideas suddenly runs dry? Ignite the conversation by telling a joke, sharing the latest office gossip or some bizarre news. Chatting about senseless things helps spark ideas in new directions.

Never Say Never

'It's never going to work. They'll never buy it.' Negativity kills creativity. Cynicism is not constructive. Surround yourself with positive-thinking people. Stay optimistic. This will liberate your mind to believe in infinite possibilities.

Start from the End

We always tend to overcomplicate the process. Before you start thinking about ideas, focus on the end result. What do you want your solution to achieve? What do you want people to feel after they hear your idea?

Begin a Conversation

Create a two-way dialogue with customers. They want to be heard and like to be involved. Start a community or a movement. Soon, you will learn more about your customers and their problems than you've ever known before.

Forget the Budget

Small budgets can sometimes constrain your thinking. Keep possibilities open by thinking big. Get the big idea first then see how you can scale it. Ironically, it's often the smallest budgets that deliver the most efficient solutions—like the Carl's Jr. example I wrote about earlier.

Find Analogs

Draw comparisons with things that are similar. If your ideation is about simplifying a process, what else do you think is simple? Tying your shoelaces is simple. Find relatable things that make connections to the problem you're trying to solve.

That Wasn't So Painful. . . or Was it?

Are you still with me? Of course you are, you brave soul. But I fear we may have lost a few readers because some of my ideation techniques can sound a little dangerous. Stink bombs? Really? Yes. Really. Did you manage to absorb these techniques easily? Or are you currently reeling like a parent on a rollercoaster after eating a stale hot dog?

Whichever way you feel, one thing is for sure. Your new brain is now filled with lots of ideation tricks. You know how to drain your brain and start with the worst ideas. You've learnt how to hijack and steal ideas. Your new favourite expression is 'What if . . .?' And you know how to force an idea in both random and opposing ways.

Congratulations. You now have a new brain that works like mine. But I'd like to reiterate one thing. These brainstorming techniques are the ones I use on a daily basis. If you use them, you'll think just like me. This is not an exhaustive list of how to come up with ideas. There are literally hundreds of other techniques you could try. So if my way is still not enough for you, at the end of this book I will recommend other books you can read that have even more techniques in them.

Soon I will reveal the final part of the puzzle, and explain the *process* you need to follow to put this knowledge to good use. But first, a few words of wisdom from another ideation legend.

Think left and think right and think low and think high. Oh, the Thinks you can think up if only you try.

Dr Seuss (Theodore Geisel) [57]

Interview with INNOVATION LEADER Valerie Madon

Before we wrap up this section on brainstorming techniques, let's hear from Valerie Madon, Chief Creative Officer APAC, McCann Worldgroup, who formerly worked at META, as the director of Creative Shop, SEA and emerging markets. During her career she has won awards at Cannes Lions, D&AD, One Show, London International, Effies, Spikes Asia, Webby's and ADFEST. Additionally, Valerie has been a judge at Cannes Lions, One Show, New York Festival and Spikes Asia and a Jury President for D&AD.

Guan: *Hi Valerie. As a global innovation leader, how important is creative conflict in the creative process?*
Valerie: Creative conflict is very important. It's the discomfort that makes the idea provocative and interesting.

Guan: *How would you describe the process of creative conflict?*
Valerie: It's often spontaneous and illogical, but your gut will tell you if it's right. Mashing up different ideas can give you an unexpected twist, but be careful, not every mash-up feels right.

Guan: *In marketing, 'disruption' describes using experimental tactics to challenge the status quo. How important is disruption?*
Valerie: That's what good advertising or communication does. To disrupt and get attention, instead of going with the flow and being unnoticed.

Guan: *Robots are taking over our jobs. What creative skills can humans use to compete against our shiny metal colleagues?*
Valerie: Algorithms are based on logic. So it's emotion that sets us apart from robots. We should tap into emotions for insights to engage people.

Guan: *What's the hardest part of learning to collide ideas?*
Valerie: To mash unexpected ideas together, the hardest part is being brave and unconditioned like a child. It's hard to not be logical.

Guan: *What's your favourite technique to collide ideas?*
Valerie: My favourite way to collide ideas is a place, not a technique. I like to brainstorm in an art museum, or somewhere that evokes freedom of expression, to put myself in the right frame of mind.

Guan: *How do you create a culture of collaboration within a company?*
Valerie: Test as many ideas with your colleagues as possible and be very open for them to build on them.

Guan: *What are the dangers of collaboration?*
Valerie: Losing the core of the idea and being too complicated after everyone's input.

Guan: *What was the best campaign solution you've done using creative conflict?*
Valerie: In 2022, I worked with my team in India to create 'The Killer Pack', where we turned packaging waste into something useful.

Guan: *Can you explain the idea behind 'The Killer Pack'?*
Valerie: Our client made mosquito repellent coils to fight mosquitoes inside the home. But the real problem was outside. Garbage collection points were acting as the main breeding grounds. To help fight mosquitos outside the home, we changed the packaging of the coil. We replaced it with 100 per cent biodegradable packaging lined with *Bacillus thuringiensis*, which kills mosquito larvae. After you've thrown away the packaging, it continues to kill mosquito larvae outside the home.

Guan: *Cool idea. What's a great fish-out-of-water solution that you love?*
Valerie: The 'Fearless Girl' statue is one of the most significant pieces of work that surprised me at the time of launch, but also remains timeless and impactful today.

Guan: *What advice would you give to someone learning about creative conflict?*
Valerie: Avoid the obvious solutions. If it's not weird, keep trying.

Guan: *Thank you, Valerie.*

Valerie nailed it when she says we need to trust our gut instinct, learn to avoid the obvious and embrace the discomfort that makes ideas provocative and interesting. And she reminds us the hardest part is thinking like a child. It's hard to not think logically, but it is this illogical, emotional thinking that will keep us one step ahead of the algorithms. Now that you've made it this far, you may feel you have everything you need to ideate like a professional. But there's still one last thing you need to learn.

While it's true the techniques you have gained will help you come up with great ideas, they must be used carefully. To get the most out of them, you must follow a process. Now I realize having a process doesn't sound very creative, but it's just a way of setting the parameters for ideation, so you can reach your destination and solve your objective efficiently.

The right process will stop you from falling off the wrong cliff. So make sure you take notes in the next chapter. Tighten those straps, hold on to the safety rope and try not to poke any poisonous snakes. It's time we discussed the seven-step ideation process that I like to call . . . COLLIDE!

Chapter Eight

A RECIPE FOR DESTRUCTION

(Where I reveal my seven-step process
to create explosive ideas).

65 MILLION YEARS AGO...

C.O.L.L.I.D.E
(The Seven Steps to a Great Idea)

The final stage of your journey is to learn the process of creative conflict. And I'll be using the asteroid that destroyed the dinosaurs 65 million years ago to illustrate my points. While it may seem obvious to some, you'd be surprised how many people never use a process and can't understand why they never have great ideas. Luckily, you're one of the clever ones and know that having a logical process is the sure-fire way to success. You appreciate that even when you're working on ideas that may be illogical, there must always be a logical process for it to be effective.

And as an aside, please accept my warmest compliments on making it this far. Not everyone could. And not everyone did. But you have proven yourself worthy and are ready to take on the last challenge. If this were a video game, it would be the boss level. The one where you use all the skills you've gained to overcome the final hurdle to victory. But don't worry. Unlike normal boss levels, this section is probably the easiest to master. If you have understood and remembered all the lessons so far, then you have acquired all the knowledge necessary to understand the process of turning ideas into innovations.

Every step of your journey with me has been leading up to this. I've shown you what creative conflict is and why it's important. You've managed to change your brain to think like mine. You've learnt how to play well with others. And you've got a few ideation tricks up your sleeve. So far, so good.

While the previous chapters have focused on the techniques and methods to come up with ideas, the next section is all about the process. From the preparations you need to complete before ideation, right up to the execution of a completed idea.

It's time to learn to C.O.L.L.I.D.E.

This acronym stands for Context, Opportunity, Learn, Leverage, Ideate, Develop and Execute. It's my tried and true process for solving any business problem. And while the individual sections of the C.O.L.L.I.D.E. processes may seem generic or obvious, that doesn't mean they are not valuable. It has been my experience that only true ideation professionals use them properly. And since you have now joined this prestigious group, I expect you will also use this process to ensure your ideation is world-class. Missing even one step will inevitably lead to ideation failure. And not the good kind!

Crashing ideas together is not simply a free-for-all, although it can feel like that sometimes. There's actually a method to the madness. If you want ideas to be both fresh and effective, you need to follow a rigorous process. First, and foremost, you need to understand the project and gather relevant information. Understanding both the context and the environment. What exactly is the problem and what do you want the solution to achieve? The next step is to find the opportunity, or the insight, that will act as your secret weapon. This will help you set a goal, or what I like to think of as a roadmap, guiding you to your final destination. It will be the GPS for your thinking. Then, and only then, will you be ready to ideate. To smash things together in a frenzy of creativity, never resting until your brain is fried, or you have discovered a new idea. But even then, there's no time to rest on your laurels.

The last step is to review the work, refining your thinking as you go. And if you have truly found a world-class, breakthrough idea . . . you must test it ruthlessly. Putting it through a bunch of torture tests. Attempting to break the idea in every way that's relevant. If it survives, and most ideas won't survive this part, you can then put the idea into action.

Many people don't know how important having a process is to successful ideation. You are not one of those people. Following this process, which at times will seem boring or obvious, will give you the best chance of finding an idea that will change everything forever. An idea that will change the world and change your life, and the one that will make you immortal.

So grab my hand one last time. And try not to squeeze as hard as you did in the previous chapters; I have delicate fingers. I promise there are no dangers ahead that I know of, but you never know what might come up. It might be safer to leave the lights on. Just in case.

Step 1: Context

Before embarking on a project that involves creative conflict, the first step of the process is to understand the project. And the environment, or context, it will exist in. You must define the business problem, or customer need that you're trying to solve. Don't assume you understand the project already. If you begin a project wearing a blindfold, how can you expect to see? The knowledge you currently have may be out of date. There is always new information to discover that will change your understanding.

Keep your eyes open. Dig around and gather information about your project, both internally and externally. How is your company currently solving the problem? How do your competitors solve it? How do your customers feel about what you do? What is the business and social environment you are working in? What are the existing parameters for the project? What are you trying to fix? How does the project fit in with your company's overall objectives?

Look for patterns in the data. Make sure you have a complete understanding of the limiting conditions, restrictions and optimization criteria. You can't think outside the box until you know what kind of box you're in. Find out what works, what doesn't and see if you can find any missed opportunities. Knowing where you've been allows you to see where you need to go. Then, once you have a complete understanding of the status quo, you'll be ready to grab a sledgehammer and smash it to bits.

Step 2: Opportunity

The context has been established and a problem defined. Now it's time to find all the good places to exploit. Where can opportunity be found? This second step involves gathering the intelligence needed to work on the project. The more information you have, the easier it will be to find connections later.

Be a vacuum cleaner and suck up all the useful information. Find your facts from a range of trusted sources. To become all knowing, you must ask the right questions—who, what, why, when, where and how. Look at examples from the past and present. Observe. Look at technology—old and new. Do a S.W.O.T. (strengths, weaknesses, opportunities and threats) analysis. And listen to your customers. They are your greatest source of unvarnished opinions. Check your assumptions of what the customers need. Try to understand what their real problem is. Make a visual mood board of how your customers feel.

If you do this, it will soon become clear to you where the opportunities lie. You will find possible directions that offer a strong chance of success. It may not show you the solution, but it will give you a benchmark for success. You can use these benchmarks as something to aim for, or something to exceed.

Remember. Gather as much information as you can. This will enable you to find more connections when you begin to brainstorm. And the more connections you have, the easier it will be to spot an opportunity.

Step 3: Learn

Once you have a thorough understanding of the context and the opportunity, the third step in the process is to learn about the specific task at hand.

You need to begin by carrying out a full review of all the intelligence you've gathered. Analyse the information in relation to your specific project. What is the problem that needs solving? Who is the end user? What is the budget? What is the timeframe? What are you aiming to deliver? Once you have a clear understanding of the problem and its parameters, you will be able to define your end goal. This is the destination you're trying to reach. The place you'd like to be when the project is over.

If you've managed to gather high-quality information and you've studied it well, then you'll have a good understanding of the problem, the context and the opportunity. Armed with this information, you can devise an end goal that is both ambitious and achievable. But be warned, my friend, a poorly defined end goal will only lead to failure. Think of it like a broken GPS that takes you to the wrong destination. A well-defined end goal, on the other hand, is like a shining beacon guiding you through dangerous waters towards a safe harbour. It provides a destination that everyone can agree on, and use, as a measure of success when the project is over.

Before you start ideating, have a tangible outcome in mind. After all, if you don't know where you're going, you'll never know if you'll get there.

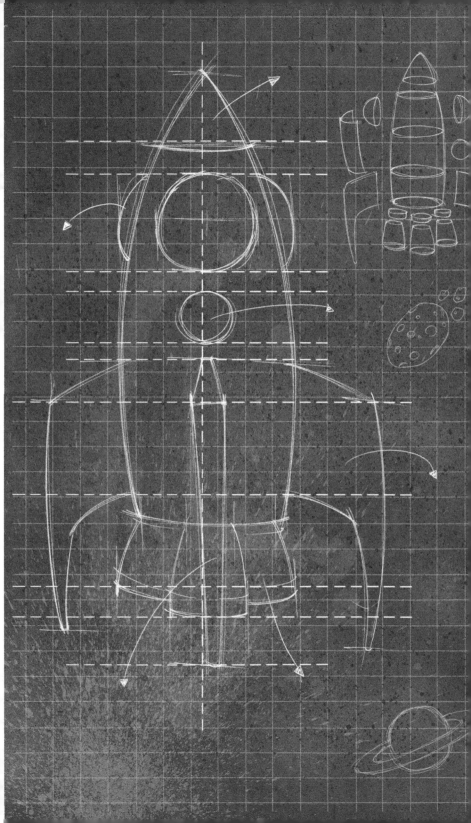

Step 4: Leverage

The fourth step in this process is to make a plan of action for your ideation session. This is where we think strategically to find the leverage for our project. What can you use from everything you've learnt to reach your end goal? After all, there's no point in gathering and studying all this information if you're not going to analyse it to form a strategy.

Leverage is about summarizing your point of view, finding the strength in your thinking and deciding what you're going to attempt. Leverage is where you develop insights, directions or themes to focus on during your ideation.

What are you hoping to achieve? How much time will you spend? How will you measure the success of the ideation? What is the output you are expecting to generate? What is the timeframe? These are just some of the questions you will need to think about to ensure productive ideation.

To reach your end goal, an effective brainstorming session needs leverage to build a strong plan. A strong plan is single-minded. So try not to clutter it up with too many objectives. One objective is the right amount. Sometimes there may be more, but they need to be secondary to your primary objective.

Once you have your leverage, you're ready to play. It's time to assemble your gladiators and head into the arena. Make sure you've got a helmet and a shield, because on the next page, we're finally going to break some stuff.

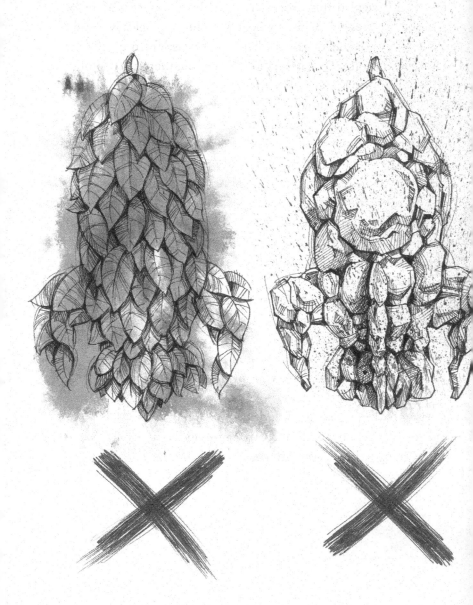

Step 5: Ideate (Break stuff)

The fifth step in the process is ideation. This is my favourite part of colliding ideas. This is where the magic happens. The place we come up with ideas, either by ourselves or preferably with others. This is the moment we've been waiting for. The moment we smash ideas together to find something new. The moment we get to break stuff. Prepare to release the Kraken!

Gather your team and meet in your dangerously safe space. Face-to-face is best, but online can work too. Present your plan to the team. Share the problem, context and opportunity available. Share the end goal based on what you've learnt and the leverage you've found. Then find a partner to do the ideation dance with. And start dancing (I mean thinking, of course).

As you brainstorm together, apply the techniques you've learnt earlier in this book to start colliding effectively. Try different ways to ideate. Generate lots of ideas. Bounce ideas off each other to make them stronger. Document the good ones (scribbles are fine). And cluster ideas in similar directions. But don't lose sight of the big picture. Don't get bogged down in the details. Remind yourself that you're looking for an idea. The execution of the idea is not important, yet. The important thing is to generate as many ideas as you can.

And if, at any stage, you find yourself having fun while colliding ideas, then rest assured, you know you're doing it right. Let the smashing begin.

ROCKET SHIP

DESCRIPTION:

BUILD THE ROCKET SHIP TO
SAVE DINOSAURS FROM EXTINCTION

Step 5 continued: (Presentation is everything)

The difference between people who succeed in ideation and those that don't has nothing to do with brainpower. It all comes down to presentation skills. A poor idea that is well presented can look great. And a great idea poorly presented will look average. Presentation is everything.

When showing your ideas to other people, you want them to see the magic of your thinking. And this can lead to overcooking presentations and making them far more complex than necessary. For other people to embrace and understand your idea, clarity of presentation is key. The simpler you make your presentation, the easier it will be for others to understand it.

A good way to clarify thinking and make presenting easier is to follow a standard format. I like to present my ideas using three elements—a title, a description and a visual. When writing the title, I think of how to summarize the new idea in five words or less. Then in the description, I try to explain what the new idea is in one sentence. Last, for the visual, I use a quick sketch or a photo to show what the new idea looks like, what it does or how it works.

This is a very simple, yet easy-to-understand format to share ideas. After you have a few ideas, you can quickly put them in this standard format, share them with everyone and then continue thinking. Once you've exhausted your brain, or the coffee pot is empty, it's time to develop the ideas.

METAL

Step 6: Develop

The sixth step in the process is to develop and hone your thinking. So far, your ideas have been kept warm and safe in your loving arms. Now it's time to review them, exposing them to the harsh light of logic. Some will make it through alive. But most are blissfully unaware they are heading for certain doom. Try to think objectively as you review the work. You'll fail, but at least you'll think a bit less subjectively. Has it solved the business problem or customer need? Is the solution new, or unexpected? Is it feasible?

I often find it's helpful to group ideas into three categories—Safe, I Love It and Scary. The first category—Safe—is for ideas that solve the problem with a predictable or incremental change. These ideas get the job done without rocking the boat. And sometimes, maintaining the status quo is all a company needs. The next category—I Love It—is for ideas that offer unpredictable solutions and powerful results. These are the award-winning ideas needed by companies wanting to grow. And the last category is Scary. These are the ideas that blow my mind. The impossible ideas. The ones that won't just increase sales, but will change the industry forever. These ideas are rare, but usually the kind employed by industry leaders.

When reviewing ideas with others, try not to talk about the ideas you don't like. This can be unproductive and often hurts feelings. Instead, look for ideas you do like, and discuss those. Have they been fully formed? Do they need more thought? Stay on track by only reviewing the good work and let unworkable ideas die naturally.

If you haven't quite solved it yet, go back to step five and IDEATE some more. But if you're feeling excited and you think you've got a world-beating idea, head to the last step and birth this idea into the world.

Step 7: Execute

At long last, after quite an adventure, you're ready to execute. This is the final step in the process, where you put the idea into action. You've made it past the dangers of ideation, so it should be smooth sailing from here. But will it be? We're about to send our idea down the very slippery slope of execution. There are new dangers ahead. And some are fatal. *Is this a good time to tell you the brakes aren't working?*

That's right. Your ideas aren't safe yet. It's time to put your ideas to the test, to prove they're both breakthrough and achievable. First, you need to identify the right parts to test. Create a visual or build a prototype. Make lots of prototypes and torture them. Be ruthless. Test them under the least favourable conditions.

If your idea seems to work, refine the idea by sharing and gathering feedback. Test it with colleagues who know about your project. Test it with customers. They're your best source of honest opinion. If it looks doable, test it with production. Get it evaluated and work out the logistics. Make sure it's feasible. If your idea needs more thinking, go back to step five and try again. Rinse and repeat as necessary. But, if you have followed the C.O.L.L.I.D.E. process properly, and your idea has passed all the tests, it's time to show the bosses.

Then, when they say yes, you can implement your idea. Receive the accolades. Get the big bonus. And change the world.

The Ride is Almost Over

Don't worry about those cuts and bruises. I'm sure the bleeding will stop soon. At least you're still relatively intact. Congratulations. You have faced many fears with passion and bravery and you have conquered the ideation process known as C.O.L.L.I.D.E. Not everyone made it this far. There were many dangers to face and I fear we may have lost a few good souls along the way. But you? You didn't perish. You're a survivor. You made it. Your natural resilience kept you going even when it seemed dark indeed. Well done. I always knew you could do it.

You are now an ideation expert. And you are not the same as you were before. You've changed your brain and play well with others. You know how to brainstorm and how to follow the seven steps of ideation. You begin each ideation session by analysing your environment and finding the best place to exploit. You understand how to gather information and make a plan. And you realize that once you've come up with ideas, you must hone your thinking and put the ideas into action.

You are now fully ready and able to ideate like a professional. But knowing how something is done is not the same as being good at something. Yes, you now have the basic starter kit for ideation, but there is a long path ahead of you, to become a world champion. To get good at ideation, you will need to practise, practise and practise some more. And then, when you're very good at it, you may just become immortal.

*You can't wait for inspiration; you
have to go after it with a club.*

Jack London [58]

Interview with SOCIAL MEDIA SENSATION
Ng Ming Wei

Before we become immortal, let's hear from a Singapore expert in all-things viral. Boom Digital Media founder Ming Wei, @mingweirocks, is one of Southeast Asia's most followed TikTok creators and has created comedy skits and videos that have gained more than 15 billion views. With 35 million followers on social media, Ming Wei is the most followed TikTok, YouTube and Facebook video creator in Singapore.

Guan: *As a content creator, how do you use creative conflict in your story process?*
Ming Wei: We like to use opposite ideas. Like smashing two things into one. When we come up with ideas for content, I think opposing ideas are the ones that have the best views. When you want a good video, you need people to comment or engage. So if you put together two things that are opposite, it will definitely get people talking about it.

Guan: *How do you think of ideas?*
Ming Wei: We start by being relatable, because if people cannot relate, they will never watch the video. We look for everyday things like using chopsticks or brushing your teeth. And then we make it more creative. If we get stuck, we try to do the opposite. Like what is the opposite thing that people might do? Something uncomfortable. That's how we make people feel conflicted. This makes people want to engage more.

Guan: *What do you mean something opposite? Can you give me an example?*
Ming Wei: Say you're making your breakfast. Do you put the cereal in first, followed by the milk? If you put the milk in first, people will have a strong reaction. They will take sides. When you

do opposite things, you do something disruptive. For example, should pineapple go on pizza? People have strong beliefs about this. So, if there's a conflict between two groups, we will make use of this conflict.

Guan: *Do you test ideas to make sure they work?*
Ming Wei: Every once in a while, I try a new concept to see how it works. If it doesn't work, then I will show it to kids and watch when they scroll away. Do they stop at the video? What makes them want to stop? I'm watching different age groups. I break it down to see what makes it watchable and universal across all ages. If you overcomplicate stuff, you might start missing your audience.

Guan: *You have a video on YouTube with over 575 million views—Using CHOPSTICKS Be Like . . . #shorts @mingweirocks. How did creative conflict play a part in making the clip?*
Ming Wei: The best content is smashed pranks. They always do well. I noticed people on social media were watching clips of kids pranking parents and filming their reaction. So I reversed the rule. We also research what's popular. Eggs have always been popular. And people always make fun of how difficult gripping the chopsticks can be if you're not Asian. So we thought, if we mix it all together, it can be quite funny. But the thing is, it's not just catching the egg. The clip wouldn't do as well. We wanted to add a twist to it. The son thinks the egg is still fresh and eats it. But, actually, it's very dirty already.

Guan: *Do you have any advice for someone learning about creative conflict?*
Ming Wei: Just think out of the box. Don't limit yourself. A lot of people only focus on what's been done before. But the most creative idea is the one people haven't done before. And it's not something you can sit down to plan. It's very hard to kick-start

something, if you don't know the process. So step one is to just keep doing stuff. The more you do, the better you get. I started by following trends. Then I realized I can add my own twist to it. And once you find some success, it motivates you. It keeps you going. The hardest thing is to start, but once you begin, you just need to keep the ball rolling.

Guan: *Thanks, Ming Wei.*

Those are some terrific tips from Ming Wei. He uses opposing ideas to create conflict, but makes sure they are relatable so viewers will connect. He thinks outside the box to find an idea that has never been done before. And he doesn't overcomplicate things, because if you overcook an idea, it gets burnt and doesn't taste very good.

Coming up in the penultimate chapter—the secret to immortality.

Chapter Nine

BIG BANG THEORISTS

(Where I show you collisions that
changed the course of history).

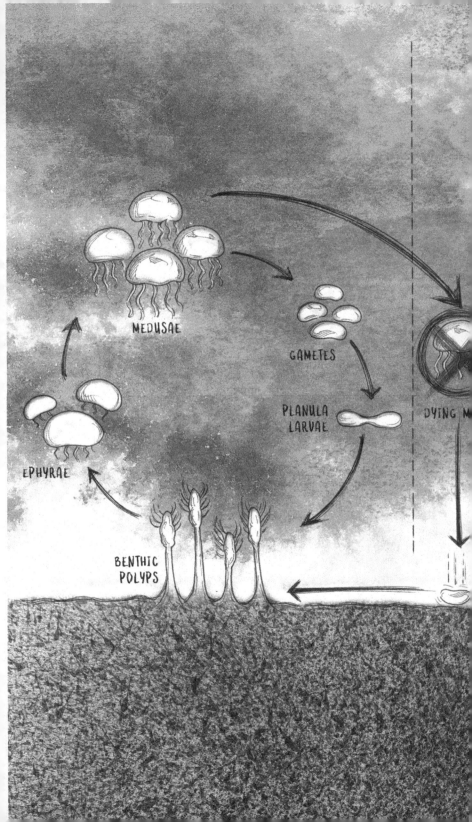

The Secret to Immortality

Throughout history, there are stories of people seeking the secret to immortality. Stories of a mythical Fountain of Youth, that restores the youth of anyone who drinks or bathes in it, have been told for thousands of years in many cultures. Modern charlatans continue to sell elixirs, potions and pills that promise to extend life. And some people have their bodies cryogenically frozen (after death) in the hope they can be brought back to life in the future. Even Sir Isaac Newton spent time trying to create the mythical Philosopher's Stone, a substance said to bestow immortality.

As it happens, there is one species that has managed to find the secret. And, sadly, it's not us. This species lives, not on earth, but under the ocean. It's a jellyfish. That's right. A jellyfish holds the secret to immortality. Who would have guessed? The scientists call it *Turritopsis dohrnii*, which is hard to say if you're drunk. And this clever little species is 'biologically immortal'. Like other jellyfish, it goes through various life stages, but, if it faces any kind of survival stress, it can revert to an earlier stage and repeat the process. Like a frog that can turn itself back into a tadpole. Unless killed by accident, or by a predator, these jellyfish can theoretically live forever.

But I'm not a jellyfish, and I'm fairly sure you're not one either. So how can we live forever? I'm glad you asked. One of the best things about coming up with ideas is the chance for immortality. To discover an innovation so great, your name goes down in the history books.

On the following pages are some illustrative examples where great thinkers used creative conflict to discover new ideas. And became immortal in the process.

THE HAPPY ACCIDENT: Super Soaker

The Super Soaker is a great example of ideation by accident. In the 1980s, water pistols were practically useless. Unable to squirt much water, or squirt very far. As someone who grew up with them, I can tell you, they weren't much fun.

Then the Super Soaker came along and changed everything. It used a sophisticated air-pressure system to squirt water out further and faster than ever before. The mayhem created was intense. You were never safe in a water fight ever again. It was a kid's dream toy.

And it all came from a happy accident by NASA engineer Lonnie Johnson. He was testing a new type of heat pump that used water as a coolant and discovered it was fun to shoot concentrated streams of water from the pump. So he created the Super Soaker as a simple, fun way to show others how his heat pumps actually worked.

On behalf of millions of children worldwide, thank you, Lonnie.

PROBLEM/NEED
Existing water pistols were practically useless.

BREAKTHROUGH MOMENT
Noticing it was fun to shoot concentrated streams of water.

SOLUTION
The discovery of the Super Soaker changed water fights forever.

THE FAILED EXPERIMENT: Artificial skin

Artificial skin is a great example of ideation by failure. In 1969, Dr John Burke invited MIT Professor Ioannis Yannas to his paediatric burns ward in Boston. There, Burke showed Yannas how bandages were incapable of sealing large damaged areas. This meant patients with extensive burns often died.

Yannas agreed to help develop a bandage that would close wounds and help patients heal. They tried a range of materials, but each failed to speed up the healing process. Their last test, with collagen polymers, actually made healing slow down. It was worse than failure. Or was it? Instead of moving past this failure, they decided to find out why. They discovered that while scars weren't forming as they had hoped, the test animals were actually growing new skin.

The 'failed' experiment taught them how to make human skin regenerate and led to artificial skin. This has revolutionized the treatment of burns victims, leading to vastly improved rates of survival.

PROBLEM/NEED
Burns victims had low rates of survival, as damage couldn't heal.

BREAKTHROUGH MOMENT
Deciding to explore why an experiment failed so badly.

SOLUTION
The discovery of artificial skin vastly improved survival rates.

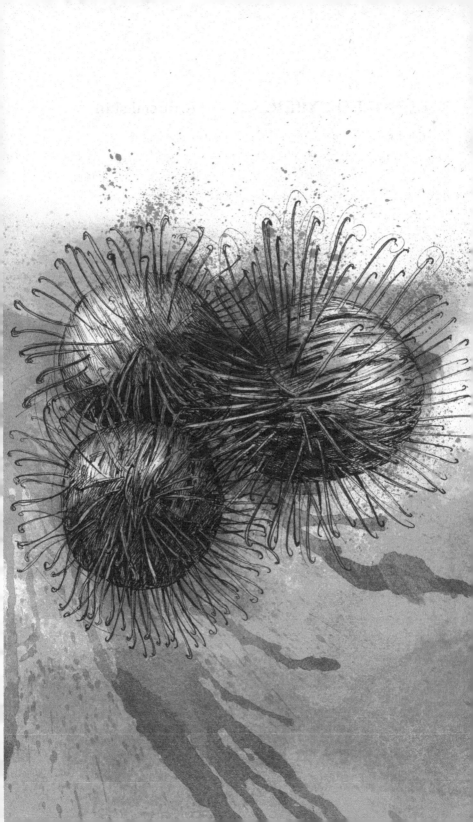

THE RANDOM OBSERVATION: Velcro

Velcro is a great example of ideation by observation. It's also a reminder that if you stay permanently curious, unexpected collisions can lead to great ideas.

In the 1940s, a Swiss electrical engineer called George de Mestral went on a hunting trip with his dog. When he returned, he noticed his dog was covered in burrs from the burdock plant. Curious to find out why the burrs stuck to the dog's fur, de Mestral put a burr under a microscope and discovered they were covered in little hooks.

That was all the inspiration he needed to create a fabric that simulated the burrs' hooks, and combine it with a fabric that had loops. It took many years to get right—almost two decades—but de Mestral finally had a product that worked, and Velcro debuted in the 1960s. Since then, it has become an extremely useful fastener, especially in clothing. It's even been used on the moon.

PROBLEM/NEED
Buttons and zippers weren't very functional fasteners.

BREAKTHROUGH MOMENT
Deciding to explore why burrs stuck to a dog's fur.

SOLUTION
The discovery of Velcro made clothes easy to fasten and unfasten.

SIR ALEXANDER FLEMING
DISCOVERED PENICILLIN.

THE HAPPY ACCIDENT: Penicillin

Before antibiotics were invented, there was no effective treatment for infections such as pneumonia, gonorrhoea and rheumatic fever. If you had blood poisoning from a scratch, doctors could do little but wait and hope.

In 1928, Alexander Fleming—Professor of Bacteriology at St Mary's Hospital London—was talking to a colleague when he noticed an area around a fungus on an agar plate in which the bacteria did not grow. He decided to find out why and, in the process, discovered penicillin. While Fleming could see penicillin's ability to kill a wide range of bacteria, he couldn't find a way to turn it into a practical therapeutic.

That happened over ten years later, when Howard Florey, Ernst Chain and their colleagues at Sir William Dunn School of Pathology at Oxford University turned penicillin from a laboratory experiment into a lifesaving drug. Their research led to the introduction of antibiotics that continue to save millions of lives each year. But this discovery would never have happened were it not for Fleming's observant eye and curious mind.

PROBLEM/NEED
Before the 1940s, infections had no effective treatment, and were often deadly.

BREAKTHROUGH MOMENT
Observing bacteria missing from where they should have been growing.

SOLUTION
The discovery of penicillin led to antibiotics that save millions each year.

THE RANDOM OBSERVATION: X-Rays

Before X-Ray machines were invented, medical problems like broken bones and tumours were all diagnosed by physical examination and a doctor's best guess. As you can imagine, there were many times when these doctors guessed poorly.

Then, on 9 November 1895, a German physics professor named Wilhelm Conrad Roentgen made an incredible discovery. He was experimenting with the conduction of electricity through low-pressure gases using fluorescent tubes, when he discovered a mysterious 'ray' capable of making a barium-coated screen fluoresce a few metres away. Objects placed between the tube and the screen cast shadows, including the bones of his hand. He tried replacing the screen with a photographic plate, and the X-ray was born.

Since then, the X-ray has revolutionized the ways we detect diseases, from cancers to broken bones. We even use it to find cracks in everything from aircraft wings to nuclear reactors.

PROBLEM/NEED
Physicians could not detect disease or injuries hidden within the body.

BREAKTHROUGH MOMENT
Deciding to investigate a strange side-effect from an unrelated experiment.

SOLUTION
The discovery of X-rays created an accurate way to detect disease and injuries.

JÜRG MARMET

No One Remembers Who Came Second

Have you ever heard of Jürg Marmet? In 1956, he was part of the second team to reach the summit of Mount Everest. Only those who get there first, become immortal.

Only those that risk going too far can possibly find out how far one can go.

T.S. Eliot [59]

Interview with CREATIVE ENGINEER
Joe Braithwaite

You've learnt the secret to immortality, but before you get to the conclusion of this book, let's take one last short break and hear from Joe Braithwaite. With a degree in Product Design Engineering, Joe has worked for over twenty years on iconic brands such as Gillette, Guinness, VISA and Tiger Beer. Now working at Google as head of Creative Works, Southeast Asia, Joe works with brands to explore creative uses of the tech giant's platforms, insights and technologies. He describes it as the alchemy of combining art with science.

Guan: *Hi Joe. When did you first learn how to crash ideas together to make new ones?*
Joe: For me, the art of crashing ideas together stems from first crashing disciplines together. My father is an architect, which led me to study both physics and art. It was during high school that the power of blending diametrically opposed forces (art and science) was revealed to me.

Guan: *What's the hardest part of learning to mash up ideas?*
Joe: Wrapping your head around the core concept. We're trained all our lives to put the right things in the right place. So to suddenly pull down the silos and experiment, goes against the grain of most of our education.

Guan: *What can I do to train my brain?*
Joe: Play a few easy games of juxtaposition. Grab two elements, images or songs at random and try to combine them in a new and unique way. Doing this a few times a week will train the muscle.

Guan: *How do you create a culture of collaboration within a company?*
Joe: The secret sauce to collaboration is a bulletproof culture built on respect, trust and fun.

Guan: *What are the dangers of collaboration?*
Joe: For me it would be 'groupthink'. By gathering a lot of people togethcr in a team, there is a danger of wanting to please everyone all the time, and thus the idea becomes vanilla. Again, there's a classic quote from Gilbert K. Chesterton that says, 'I've searched all the parks in all the cities and found no statues of committees.'

Guan: *How important is creative conflict in the creative process?*
Joe: Creative ideation is rarely, if ever, linear. The light bulb of inspiration can come in many forms. But one of the richest veins is to take existing ideas and smash them together to see what they can create. A great idea I saw was 'Gig In The Sky' with Jamiroquai. People had been to concerts. People had been on aeroplanes. But no one had been to a gig at 30,000 feet before.

Guan: *How important is disruption?*
Joe: In today's age, disruption is everything. People lead busy lives, they have thousands of brands, screens and people vying for their attention. If you're not disrupting, how on earth do you hope to capture and hold attention? A famous line from a planner I work with is 'Planners should worry less about being right, and more about being interesting.'

Guan: *When problem-solving with creative conflict, what's the most important thing to remember?*
Joe: Channel the conflict to the idea, not each other. I've seen a quote 'Be hard on the work, not each other', so remember that conflict doesn't mean arguing with each other.

Guan: *Robots are taking our jobs. What creative skills do human employees need?*

Joe: No matter how sophisticated, machine learning is still drawing on—and amalgamating—the sum of human knowledge. It's producing the mean response to a human request. So we have two jobs, the first is the easy one—we are the prompt, and without us there are no instructions to the machine. The second is more exciting. We are the element of surprise, the curiosity and the inspiration in the creative process—'the spark'.

Guan: *What advice would you give to someone learning about creative conflict?*

Joe: Think like a military strategist. The element of surprise often trumps all other tactics.

Guan: *Thanks Joe.*

What I love about this interview is that Joe teaches us the importance of being interesting. And shows us we can reach this goal by retraining our brains to use the power of blending opposing forces. He also reminds us to be hard on the work, not each other, because a bulletproof culture is built on respect, trust and fun.

Sadly, our time together is almost over, but I have one more surprise to share with you about your new brain. Let's find out in the thrilling conclusion on the next page.

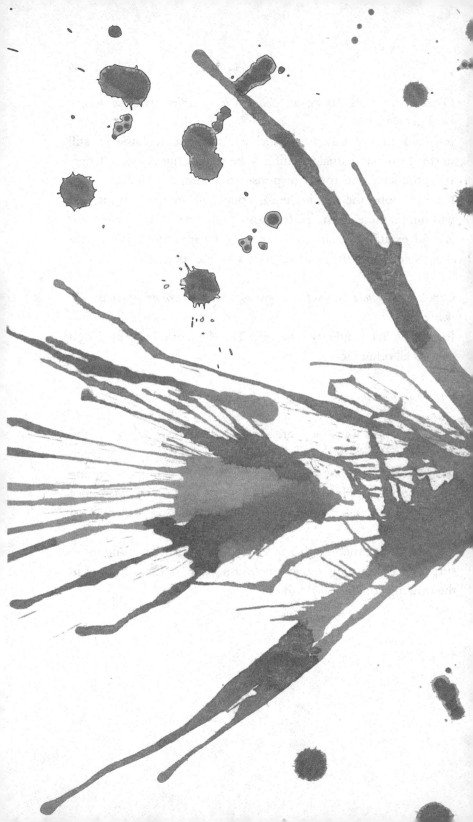

Chapter Ten

SELF
DESTRUCT
SEQUENCE
INITIATED

(Where I say goodbye and then start
to back away ... very slowly).

BEFORE

YUGO

AFTER

VENOM GT

Here's What I Did to Your Brain

The car on the top is called a Yugo. It's wrong on so many levels, I don't know where to begin. The Yugo was poorly made and prone to breakdown. It had a low speed and handled terribly. I consider it the second worst car ever made (after the Trabant).

The car on the bottom, however, is a Hennessey Venom GT. Only thirteen of these speed demons were ever produced. With a V8 Twin Turbo engine, it has a top speed of 435 kph (270 mph). If it's not the world's fastest car, it definitely comes a close second.

You may think that, before you began this book, you had a brain like a Yugo. And now, with the lessons gained, you may think your brain has been transformed into a Hennessey Venom GT. But looks can be deceiving. That's not what I did to your brain.

As I said at the beginning of this book, the truth is, you already have a beautiful brain. One that is just as powerful as anyone else's. Like most humans on this planet, you've always had a Hennessey Venom GT brain, and you've never had a Yugo brain. All I've done is dusted off the Yugo perception, cleared out the cobwebs in your brain, and given you back your childhood ability to believe the impossible.

Remember, the US military has footage of real UFOs. Scientists have theorized that it rains diamonds on Neptune. And Captain Kirk (William Shatner) has actually been to space. Anything is possible as long as you believe.

Let's Go Break Something

Congratulations on making it to the end. Not everyone did, but I knew you could. Take the time to enjoy a well-earned rest, put some Band-Aids on those paper cuts and apply ice to any bruises. And let's not forget to spare a thought for those who didn't make it this far.

You, on the other hand, are now officially an expert in the world's most powerful ideation technique! You know how to C.O.L.L.I.D.E. You know what creative conflict is, why it's important and how it works. You also know how to collide with others and have conquered the ideation process. With the knowledge you have gained, you have all the tools you need to brainstorm like a professional and discover innovative solutions to any problems you might be facing right now.

But so far, it's just been theory. Soon, it will be time for you to put that learning into practice. Remember to use your knowledge wisely. Always stay hopeful and curious about the world around you. Celebrate your wins and forget your losses. Keep a positive mindset. Ignore fear and stay passionate.

You've transformed yourself, now get out there and change the world. Start mashing ideas together. Break some stuff. Build it back stronger. Turn the lessons you've learnt in this book, into innovations in your own life. And always use your skills for the greater good. There is a 2,000-year-old adage from the story of the Sword of Damocles that many people think comes from the Marvel Comics character Spiderman. The adage says: 'With great power comes great responsibility'. Use your new power wisely. Your ideation adventure begins now.

Come to the edge.
We might fall.
Come to the edge.
It's too high!
COME TO THE EDGE!
And they came.
And he pushed.
And they flew.
Christopher Logue [60]

Recommended Reading

Are you still hungry for more knowledge? Do you want to expand your giant new brain even more? Then, you're in luck. Below is a list of other books that will help. I'd love to say I have a monopoly on creative wisdom. But sadly for me—and fortunately for you—there are many writers out there who know quite a lot more about the subject than me.

My book can help you find success with ideation, but the following books can change your life. Do yourself a huge favour and check them out. They are full of brilliant insights, wise advice and—dare I say it—even better techniques to come up with ideas. If my book has started you down a path of learning, then these books are essential reading on your journey. Devour them all.

It's Not How Good You Are, It's How Good You Want to Be
by Paul Arden (Phaidon Press, 2003)

It may surprise you to find out I don't like reading. But if you're like me and don't read that much, then this is the book for you. It tells a lot of different stories and sheds light on many different situations that define creativity as it applies to business and life. The information is presented in simple, short, wit-filled pieces with fun visuals. So it's very easy to read, in easily digestible chunks.

Packed with facts, wisdom and insights into creativity, it's a good all-round guide that's as suitable for experts as it is for newcomers. The same author wrote another great book called *Whatever You Think, Think the Opposite*.

Steal Like an Artist
by Austin Kleon (Workman, 2012)

A very well-deserved *New York Times* bestseller, *Steal Like an Artist* teaches you ten amazing principles that can transform your creative thinking. For me, this is probably the best book on this list. It's definitely my favourite for layout and design. The author's style is simple, quirky, bizarre and funky. He even doodles in the book (and as I love to mention, I am a *huge* fan of doodling).

The ideas in this book are deeply rewarding, yet anyone could read this book in one sitting. I like to keep a copy near me at all times so I can steal from it. Occasionally, I like to leave it on the coffee table to impress others. Can you tell I'm a little jealous? Another good book by the same genius author is *Show Your Work, And Keep Going.*

Creative Confidence: Unleashing the Creative Potential Within Us All
by David and Tom Kelley (Currency, 2013)

The two brothers who wrote this book are two of the world's leading experts on innovation, design and creativity. They are the advocates of 'design thinking'—the human-centred, multidisciplinary approach to innovation, which considers the needs of people, technological possibilities and requirements for success in business.

In this book, the co-founders of global design and innovation company IDEO explore some of the award-winning work they have done for clients. Take your time with this one. The wisdom in this book is the good stuff. These people don't just have a deep understanding of how good ideas are made; they also know how to make them very profitable too. Tom has also written another great book, *The Art of Innovation.*

Change by Design: How Design Thinking Transforms Organizations and Inspires Innovation

by Tim Brown (HarperCollins, 2009)

Those people from IDEO sure do love to write books. Here's another one written by their CEO, Tim Brown. In this book, he gives concrete examples of how to integrate design thinking into every level of business. Using factual examples, Brown shows how design thinking has become the default process for anyone trying to solve a business problem with a new idea. It's the framework that all great thinkers use. And increasingly, it's the framework all great businesses use.

This is a must-have book for anyone in a leadership position. It shows how design thinking is not just for designers; it's for anyone who wants to put design-thinking principles at the heart of their product or service. This one would make a good 'Secret Santa' gift for your CEO.

Creativity Inc.: Overcoming the Unseen Forces That Stand in the Way of True Inspiration
by Ed Catmull and Amy Wallace (Random House, 2014)

Want to build a creative powerhouse? Want to create a culture of innovation, never seen before in your industry? Or just want to read a fun story? Then, this is the book for you. Another *New York Times* bestseller, *Creativity Inc.* was co-written by Ed Catmull, the co-founder of Pixar Animation Studios. On a gentle, yet inspiring journey, we are taken through the world of Pixar in its early days, through its early struggles and late successes.

This book offers lots of sage advice. Mostly for managers and entrepreneurs who want to lead employees to new heights, create a culture like no other, build a business that is loved and admired and make money while doing all three.

The Doodle Revolution: Unlock the Power to Think Differently
by Sunni Brown (Portfolio, 2015)

Perhaps I've mentioned once or twice that doodling is one of my favourite things to do while trying to think of ideas. Doodling is pure magic. It's a powerful deep-thinking tool that's simple and accessible to all. Did you know that doodling integrates hand-eye coordination with your logical brain, your visual brain and your subconscious? What's not to like? Personally, I've done it since I was a teenager, getting in trouble for doodling on school textbooks. Powerful thinkers like Thomas Edison, Marie Curie and Albert Einstein were all doodlers, and that's some prestigious company to keep. The author, Sunni Brown, shows us how doodling works, and why. Well worth the price. More power to the doodle!

Where Good Ideas Come From: The Natural History of Innovation
by Steven Johnson (Riverhead Books, 2011)

This book provides the answer to the question every creative person gets asked. Where do good ideas come from? Do magical fairies anoint the chosen ones with inspiration? Or is it a natural skill we all possess? Steven Johnson, the *New York Times* bestselling author of *How We Got to Now,* answers the question with a captivating deep-dive into the sea of innovation.

Using his deep understanding of neurobiology and popular culture, Steven reveals the seven key patterns that are common for true innovation and tells an encouraging story of how we generate ideas that can help us move forward in our careers, lives and society. Read this book if you're looking for deeper, scientific insights into ideation.

Damn Good Advice (For People with Talent!): How to Unleash Your Creative Potential by America's Master Communicator
by George Lois (Phaidon Press, 2012)

George Lois is one of America's biggest creative minds and a legend in every sense of the word. Meaning it's often impossible to tell where the legend stops and the myth begins. Nevertheless, this book offers valuable insights, lessons, facts, anecdotes and loads of practical advice. Apparently, every word in it is true (according to George Lois). But I'd take each story as a fable. And while most of his wisdom was born in the last century, the advice on how to use creativity to succeed in business is timeless.

This book is easy to read and packed with short bite-size chunks of wisdom on every page. I don't usually include swearing as part of my repertoire, but *damn*, this book is good. It's the kind of book I wish I'd read when I was sixteen. You should order a copy online today.

How to Get Ideas

by Jack Foster and Larry Corby (Berrett-Koehler, 1996)

It's just what the title says. This is a book that teaches you how to have better ideas using a simple five-step process anyone can follow. Most of all, Foster shows us how having fun is part of the ideation process. How cool is that?

In fact, your mindset has a lot to do with the overall quality of your ideas and this is where the book comes to life. It teaches us how to change the way we think, so that we utilize our sense of humour, develop curiosity and visualize goals. The author also includes lots of tricks and techniques to make your brain more prone to ideas. All in all, a worthy read if you need help to change the way you approach the ideation process.

The Little Spark: 30 Ways to Ignite Your Creativity

by Carrie Bloomston (Stash Books, 2014)

Do you feel like you've lost your creative spark? Finding it harder and harder to come up with ideas? If people have been pouring cold water over your ideas for years, you may feel like your creativity has been extinguished. But do not worry, my friend.

We all carry the fire of creativity within us. Sometimes, it just needs a spark to start a raging firestorm of ideas. This book teaches you thirty ways to make sparks. And that's more than enough to get your creative engines fired up.

A very practical book, the lessons inside can be learnt in a single sitting, or you can make dog-ears on the pages and come back to it from time to time. It's the kind of book that when you're finished, you can't claim to not know how to spark creativity. And that, alone, is worth the purchase price.

The Copywriters Bible: How 32 of the World's Best Advertising Writers Write their Copy
by Alistair Crompton (RotoVision, 2000)

Since I work predominantly in advertising, I couldn't leave this one off the list. It might not be useful for all of you, but this book will be priceless to anyone who writes for a living. The writers showcased in this book were chosen because they were at the top of their game. And even though they all have the same job, reading this book helps you discover they all have different ways of solving similar problems.

It's a great demonstration of the idea that there's no 'one' way to solve a problem. You just need to learn what works for you. Which is a great piece of advice for writers, or anyone starting off in life. It was first published in 1995 under a different title (*The Copy Book*). Also by the same author is *The Craft of Copywriting*.

Acknowledgement

Writing a book has proven to be more complex than I anticipated and more fulfilling than I ever imagined. As a visual artist, writing has never been my preferred form of expression, but I've come to appreciate its beauty and have developed a comfortable writing style over time.

This progress would not have been possible without my copywriter partner, James Scanlon, who has contributed to some of the most memorable advertising campaigns I've worked on. We met in Leo Burnett Singapore in 2000 and then later in JWT, where we produced award-winning and insightful work.

To all the executive creative directors, copywriters and art directors I've worked with, thank you for the opportunity to create compelling and unexpected solutions. I'm also grateful to my clients, for giving me the privilege of helping them, as they pushed me to exceed my expectations. And to all the colleagues and friends who played a role in my journey, your contributions have been indispensable.

Jerome Joseph, your guidance, coaching and motivation have been instrumental in helping me complete this book. Your valuable insights and encouragement have driven this project and I could not have done it without you.

Wendy Ng, thank you for your exceptional organizational and coordination skills in overseeing the artwork.

To Fredrick Chua Jue Heng who illustrated this book, your striking images have illuminated my very dull words.

I'd also like to thank the members of Asia Professional Speakers Singapore. Your willingness to lend a helping hand has made this journey unforgettable. I have learned so much and am deeply grateful for your kindness.

To my three children, Ryan Tay Wei Loong, Oliver Tay Wei Yang, and Megan Sarah Tay Wei Li, you have my gratitude and appreciation for the joy and love you bring into my life. You are the light that illuminates my world and you motivate me daily to become a better person. You are the greatest gift a father could ever ask for.

I am eternally grateful to my late father, Dr Tay Chong Hai, and my late mother, Dr Gaw Yang Neo, who supported me emotionally and financially in my creative pursuits. And I want to thank my Uncle Sin Hock Gaw, who recommended the ArtCenter College of Design in Pasadena, where I learnt the fundamental principles of creativity.

To my late father and mother-in-law, Mr and Mrs Chen, you welcomed me into your family, treating me as one of your own. I am very grateful for your love and kindness, and am blessed to have you in my life. Your guidance, wisdom and support are invaluable, especially during difficult times.

Finally, to my wife and the rock of our household, Nissa Chen, I am deeply grateful and feel incredibly blessed to have you as my partner, best friend and love of my life. I treasure every moment with you and eagerly anticipate many more years of happiness and passion. Your unwavering dedication, patience and understanding have played a crucial role in helping me pursue and achieve my goals. I love you, sweetie.

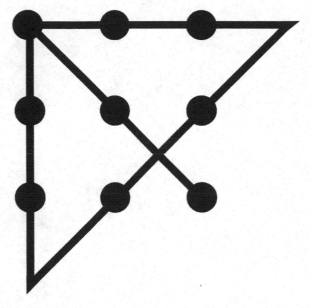

The solution to the nine-dot puzzle from page 93.

List of References

1 Edward Waldo Emerson and Waldo Emerson Forbes, 18491855, Volume 8, Year Specified for Journal Entry: 1855, 528, Houghton Mifflin Company, Boston, Massachusetts.

2 William C. Taylor, 'The Leader of the Future', interview with Ronald Heifetz, Fast Company (June 1999): 131138, http://www. fastcompany.com/magazine/25/heifetz.html

3 Mark Tungate, Adland: A Global History of Advertising, 2 Edition 2013, 70, Kogan Page.

4 M.E. Harding, The I and the not I: A study in the Development of Consciousness, 1965, p.82, Princeton University Press.

5 David Gracia, Wake up Beauty: Creativity in the art of Love, 2021, 100, Google Books.

6 World Economic Forum: The Future of Job Report 2020.

7 Jesus Sanchez, 'Pam Am ceases operations after 64 years in Sky', Los Angeles Times Business Section Dec 1991.

8 Phil Wahba & Tom Hals, 'Borders files for bankruptcy to close 200 stores', Reuters February 2011.

9 Annalyn Censky, 'Blockbuster files for bankruptcy', CNN Money September 2010.

10 Sabrina E., '41 Most Famous Marsha Blakburn Quotes', Contact Senators viewed on April 2022 https://contactsenators.com/ articles/marsha-blackburn-quotes/

11 Albert Einstein, Letter to biographer Carl Seelig 11 March 1952, library archives ETH Zurich, viewed on March 2022 from https://www. mentalfloss.com/article/518759/6-priceless-documents-reveal-key-moments-early-einsteins-career

12   Laurel Wentz, 'Volvo recruited real car crash survivors to staff its sale booths', *AdAge* April 2017.

13   Chauncey Alcorn, 'Burger King thinks mouldy Whoppers will get you to buy more burgers', *CNN Business* February 2020.

14   Mark Twain (Samuel Clemens), 'Chapters from My Autobiography', *North American Review* 1906, 61.

15   Presiding Bishop of the Church of Jesus Christ of Latter-day Saints, 2015.

16   Unknown, *The Lore and Language of Schoolchildren*, by Iona and Peter Opie, p 24-29 Oxford University Pres.

17   *Emerson In His Journals* (1982), Selected nd Edited y Joel Porte, p. 294, Harvard University Press.

18   Miles Kington, 'Heading for a Sticky End', *The Independent UK March 2003* https://www.independent.co.uk/voices/columnists/miles-kington/heading-for-a-sticky-end-112674.html

19   Gemma Chilton, 'Here are the animals REALLY most likely to kill you in Australia', *Australian Geographic* 2016, viewed on 22 March 2022 from

20   Isaac Newton, *Letter to Robert Hooke 5 February 1675*, Historical Society of Pennsylvania, Gratz Collection, viewed on 24 March 2022 from https://digitallibrary.hsp.org/index.php/Detail/objects/9792

21   'Mind wandering "Ahas" versus mindful reasoning: alternative routes to creative solutions', *Frontiers in Psychology* Vol 6, p.834.

22   Terman, Michael; Terman, 'Jiuan Su Treatment of Seasonal Affective Disorder with a High-Output Negative Ionizer' *The Journal of Alternative and Complementary Medicine* 1(1): 87–92. doi:10.1089/acm.1995.1.87.

23   Lenard, P. Über die Elektrizität der Wasserfälle , Lpz, 46584–636.

24   UK: Walker Books US: Little Brown & Co then Candlewick Press Published 1987–present. https://en.wikipedia.org/wiki/Where%27s_Wally%3F

25   Mary Lou Cook quoted in Scott E. Kauffman, *If Tomorrow Never Comes: What would you do with your last twenty-four hours?*, iUniverse June 2015.

26   Priyanka B. Carr Gregory M. Walton, 'Cues of working together fuel intrinsic motivation', *Journal of Experimental Psychology*, Stanford University.

27   Robinson, Ken, 'The Element: ow inding our assion hanges verything', *Viking Press*, New York, 2008.

28 *Worstward Ho!*irst published in Nohow On, Calder Publications, UK 1989.

29 Mueller, P.A., & Oppenheimer, D.M. 'The pen is mightier than the keyboard: Advantages of longhand over laptop note taking'. *Psychological Science*, 25, 1159–1168.

30 'Ink on Paper: Some Notes on Note Taking' *Psychological Science* January 2014.

31 Wade, Patricia Ann *Medical Student Education*. Indiana University. Web 22 September 2015.

32 Toni Morrison, *The Art of Fiction No. 134*, interviewed by Elisa Schappell and Claudia Brodsky Lacour, *The Paris Review*, Issue 1281993.

33 'Freedom from onstraints: Darkness and im llumination romote reativity', *Journal of Environmental Psychology* Volume 356780.

34 Claudia Geidel, Ketchum.com March 2013 https://www.ketchum.com/brainstorming-in-the-dark/

35 The National Institute for Play https://www.nifplay.org

36 'Evolution, Early Experience and Human Development: From Research to Practice and Policy', *Oxford University Press*, 29 November 2012.

37 Jung, C.G *Psychological Types, The collected Works of C.G. Jung*, Vol 6, Paragraph 197, Bollingen Series XX, *Princeton University Press*

38 'Attributed to Picasso, Modern Living: Ozmosis in Central Park', *TIME* Oct 1976.

39 'Darya L. Zabelina and Michael D. Psychology of Aesthetics, Creativity, and the Arts', p. 57-65, *North Dakota State University* Vol 4, No. 1.

40 'Chapter 24: Edison's Method in Inventing', *Edison: His Life and Inventions*, Volume 2, Harper & Brothers, New York.

41 *Harvard Business Review* (2019), viewed on 1 March 2022 from hJps://hbr.org/2019/09/to-overcome-your-fear-of-public-speaking-stop-thinking-about-yourself

42 Colin D. Ellis, *The Project Book The Complete Guide to Consistently Delivering Great Projects*, Wiley 2019, 124.

43 Byrne RMJ. 'The rational imagination: How people create alternatives to reality'. *MIT Press*; Cambridge, MA 2005.

44 Persuasion and the Role of Visual Presentation Support: The UM/3M Study, Volume 86, Issue 11 of *Working apers series*, University of Minnesota 1986.

45   Only (2021), viewed on March 2022 from hJps:// 2 www.
      onlymelbourne.com.au/gotye

46   *The Guardian Australian anthems* (2022), viewed on 3 March 2022 from
      hJps://www.theguardian.com/music/australia-culture-blog/2014/
      jun/24/australian-anthemsgotye-featuring-kimbra-somebody-
      that-i-used-to-know

47   https://www.businessinsider.com/oreos-super-bowl-power-
      outage-tweet-was-18-months-in-the-making-2013-3

48   Oxford English Dictionary, 2 Edition 1989.

49   Front. Psychol. 29 July 2016 https://doi.org/10.3389/fpsyg.
      2016.01116, viewed in March 20 from https://www.frontiersin.
      org/articles/10.3389/fpsyg.2016.01116/full

50   https://www.bloomberg.com/news/articles/2012-03-01/
      sprinkles-cupcakes-explains-its-24-hour-cupcake-atm

51   https://www.forbes.com/sites/micahsolomon/2018/12/23/
      how-safelite-built-a-customer-service-culture-doubled-revenue-
      by-consulting-customers-directly/?sh=2bd5c3a33390

52   https://takeashans.com/uptown-bar-buenos-aires-2/

53   Lux Magical Spell campaign for Unilever.

54   Luke Goodsell, ABC Arts, *Aaron Blabey he Bad Guys nterview*, ABC
      News, viewed on 31 March 2022 from https://www.abc.net.au/
      news/2022-03-31/aaron-blabey-the-bad-guys-interview-movie-
      adaptation-dreamworks/100951220

55   Ransom E. Olds Creates the First Automobile Assembly Line
      1897 to 1901.

56   Edward Jenner and the advent of vaccination, National Library of
      Medicine May 1983.

57   Dr Seuss, *Oh, the Thinks you Can Think!*, Penguin Random House
      1975.

58   *Practical Authorship*, Getting Into Print by Jack London 140, 143,
      The Editor Publishing Company, New York.

59   Preface to *Transit of Venus*. Poems, Black Sun Press 1931.

60   Christopher Logue 1926–2011 English poet 'Come to the edge'
      (1968). From a poster advertising an Apollinaire exhibition at the
      Institute of Contemporary Art 1969.